CROPS, PEOPLE AND IRRIGATION

CROPS, PEOPLE AND IRRIGATION

Water allocation practices of farmers and engineers

Edited by
GEERT DIEMER and FRANS P. HUIBERS

INTERMEDIATE TECHNOLOGY PUBLICATIONS 1996

Intermediate Technology Publications Ltd,
103–105 Southampton Row, London WC1B 4HH, UK

© Intermediate Technology Publications 1996

ISBN 1 85339 304 5

A CIP record for this book is available from
the British Library

Typesetting by J&L Composition Ltd,
Filey, North Yorkshire
Printed in UK by SRP, Exeter

Contents

To Jacques Slabbers

Preface

This publication was originally conceived as a translation of collected case studies published in Dutch in 1991 under the title *Irrigatietechniek en cultuur, opvattingen van boeren en ingenieurs over de verdeling van water* (Irrigation technology and culture, views of farmers and engineers on the distribution of water). The collection was edited by Jacques Slabbers and Geert Diemer with a view to comparing actual water distribution practices on irrigation schemes with received engineering notions about this process. When, in 1993, work started on the English-language version, fresh case studies were available that superseded some studies in the original 1991 collection. Consequently, it was decided to edit a new collection centred around the same theme.

The time gap between the two publications is due in part to the illness and untimely death of Jacques Slabbers. As an experienced irrigation engineer, Slabbers was well aware that many agency-managed irrigation schemes built in developing countries in the 1960s and 1970s had not fulfilled their promises of improving the livelihoods of poor farming families and had even worsened their living conditions. This observation stimulated him to rethink irrigation engineering design practices: in his youth he had chosen the irrigation specialization with a view to assisting poor Third World farmers. We therefore dedicate this enriched version to the memory of our friend and colleague.

The book reflects efforts by the Department of Irrigation and Soil and Water Conservation of Wageningen Agricultural University to understand irrigation technology in the context of its many interactions with the social and physical world. Many experts nowadays agree that much of the present disappointing performance of investments of public money in irrigation may be attributed to a lack of knowledge, not of the physical and technical aspects of irrigation, but of their impact *and* dependence on human relations. We know little about the socio-technical processes that send water from group A to group B and exclude groups C or D, or about the impact of relations between groups on the physical configuration of schemes. We hope this collection will encourage others to make more substantial contributions to this knowledge.

Geert Diemer and Frans P. Huibers
Wageningen, the Netherlands

1. Introduction[1]

GEERT DIEMER and FRANS P. HUIBERS

One of the most astonishing facts about technical development co-operation is that many agricultural experts know little about the practices they are paid to improve. Paul Richards (1985, 1986) has documented the divergence between the objectives of Sierra Leone farmers in selecting rice varieties and the rice research conducted at a nearby research station. Van der Ploeg (1989) made comparable discoveries with respect to Peruvian potato farmers and potato research, and De la Rive Box (1989) for cassava research in Jamaica.[2]

In a similar vein, irrigation engineers know little about the actual principles of distribution of water on schemes in developing countries. They often assume that on their schemes, which are mostly gravity-operated, there is no better way of distributing water than according to the rules they had in mind when they designed and built the irrigation systems. Jurriëns and De Jong (1989) surveyed the literature published between 1970 and 1985 on water management on large smallholder schemes. They found almost 1000 titles but not even one handbook or accepted analytical conceptual framework. They also noted the absence of comprehensive and clear descriptions of how in reality water is distributed and schemes are operated. Most authors were social scientists and contributions by engineers and technicians were scarce.

Since 1985, however, many attempts have been made to redress the balance, as the following sections will demonstrate.

Technical co-operation in irrigation development

The role of foreign engineers in irrigation development is primarily that of designing the scheme. Their clients are the national ministries of planning, agriculture or water, and the funding development banks. Technical criteria for the design, design alternatives and layouts are discussed with groups of officials from these bureaucracies, even when the scheme is to be farmed by local smallholders.

---

[1] This text has greatly benefited from contributions by Paul Hoogendam and Peter Mollinga.
[2] For French-speaking Africa this theme is discussed in J.-P. Olivier de Sardan and E. Paquot (ed.) 1989.

The design method broadly follows the logic of the individual investor. It is governed by a search for physical efficiency, first by calculating the crop water requirements, and second by comparing designs with respect to the water use efficiency of the subsystems. The design procedure focuses on crop and construction issues with the aim of reducing expenditure on construction, management and maintenance.

The engineers usually base their designs solely on physical data. The only social components likely to be considered are demographic information (such as the labour force) and the potential economic and financial yield of the scheme and plots. Empirical data on the diversity in make-up and dynamics of the farms, the groups of irrigators, the organizational patterns and local political structures are rarely available.

At the level of the cultivator, a single and permanent cropping pattern is usually assumed (often monoculture in schemes initiated by public agencies). As regards the choice of the size of the plot, planners often assume that all labour will be used to cultivate the irrigated plot, because they perceive rainfed cultivation as being no longer rewarding. Other implicit assumptions concern the absence of livestock, off-farm work and off-farm sources of income and of remittances from kin who have migrated.

Considering the farmers as a group, the major assumptions may be, for example, that all farmers have a similar plot, that they follow the same cropping pattern, and that the irrigation interval, duration and flow on the fields are uniform, as prescribed in the design.

In the design of the canals, it is usually assumed that water distribution and allocations will not change over time. It is also assumed that management should be eased by reducing variation in the intervals and by standardizing the water application over the growing season. Management of the scheme is necessarily centralized and farmers are assumed to take orders. If it turns out that the scheme is operated differently, it is felt that the farmers and operators need training and extension.

Reactions to shortcomings in irrigation development

It is now generally acknowledged that the 15 billion dollars that used to be poured into the irrigation subsector in less-developed countries annually have not produced more than 50 per cent of the anticipated output (Nijman 1993). In the 1960s this disappointing performance was not widely known, but engineers had already started to search for physical improvements such as extending the design to the tertiary block, improving the calculation of the water needs of crops and improving distribution structures and lining canals.

The hypothesis gained ground that the practice of limiting design to the primary and secondary canal networks was a major cause of underperformance and inefficiency. It was proposed that the tertiary level should also be designed by engineers and be built by contractors. These proposals were adopted by the donor agencies and national governments. By the 1970s the terms of reference for scheme studies routinely included the design and construction of the tertiary level. Today, many design reports even calculate and prescribe strict rotations for the distribution of water at the tertiary level.

A second technical response to the disappointing performance of schemes consisted of refining measuring techniques. These techniques have made it possible to calculate crop transpiration more accurately and to calculate agronomically optimal irrigation gifts and intervals, primarily for cash crops.

The incentive for a third change came from the advent of high-yielding varieties of rice, maize and cotton. These varieties require water applications that are administered and timed precisely to realize their potential. This development favoured the installation of measurement devices and adjustable distribution systems in the primary, secondary and tertiary canals. Automatic systems also became more popular with system managers.

However, these and other developments in the technical hardware contributed little to solving the problems encountered on irrigation schemes. In the 1970s certain leading professionals (Levine 1980, FAO 1972, and others) started to pay attention to what they described as the software of irrigation systems. Initially they focused on operation and maintenance realizing that more training was needed to help water guards and other operators to understand scheduling and to encourage farmers to use efficient field application methods, to level their fields and maintain the tertiary canals.

It was subsequently acknowledged that using an irrigation system means collaboration between people. An interest was taken in what management science had to say on crucial topics such as the collaboration between engineers and farmers and the internal operation of irrigation bureaucracies. Some donor agencies expected this focus to be sufficiently fertile to justify the establishment, in 1985, of a specialized international research centre, the International Irrigation Management Institute (IIMI).

Today, technology, operation and maintenance of main systems and management of the institutional relationships are elements of an ongoing search for responses to the disappointing output of the irrigation subsector of agriculture. These three foci pay little if any attention to studying how water is actually managed and distributed, and instead concentrate on how designers think this could be done better. Access to water as a right, and irrigation infrastructures as forms of capital, are not part of the vocabulary of the 'traditional' irrigation expert.

The hidden foundations of water distribution

Natural water courses do not necessarily flow over the most fertile fields, so people build weirs, dams, canals and other structures to redirect the water.

These hydraulic works are conceived, built and consequently owned by people or institutions. The hidden but basic legal implications of this first received attention in the 1980s in pioneering work by the rural sociologist Coward (1986a, 1986b) and a group of Cornell-based researchers.

Coward's insight was summarized in the notion of irrigation development as a process of creation of hydraulic property.[3] One cannot build facilities without establishing proprietary rights. Individuals who for their own use help build an irrigation system, either personally or through paid labour, receive a right to the water. Often, a person's contribution to the initial investment equals that person's share in the water.

Coward quotes Tamaki, who writes that in general, the function of 'terre capital' stock or 'landesque capital' is to integrate labour into land so that 'past labour' can be used to facilitate 'present labour'. When a holder of rights dies, his estate will contain his share in the capital that he, his ancestors or others created and that during his lifetime he has maintained.

Although the number of water shares may remain stable, each share may be divided into fractions, by inheritance and sale. Over time, the number of holders of rights usually increases. Any allocation of water to later shareholders, no matter how complex, may in principle be traced to the configuration of initial shares, even when the memory of the irrigators does not go back that far.

The co-owners usually unite in some kind of self-governing association. Its assemblies and elected officers define and enforce rules on how its members may exercise their rights and should execute their obligations. The latter may consist primarily of efforts to upkeep the property. People who are not co-owners are usually not allowed to contribute to the maintenance of the weir and the canals, as otherwise they may later claim that their contribution entitles them to water. Like other types of private ownership of real estate, the proprietary rights exclude other people.

Farmers who wish to join an association of owners of hydraulic property are not necessarily accepted and will somehow have to pay their share in the capital stock. They may be allowed to buy a right or be granted usufruct, on the condition that they take responsibility for the maintenance of all or part of the infrastructure for the benefit of the earlier holders of rights whose maintenance obligations they take over. In this way, by repairing and reconstructing the system, new water-right holders buy their share in the capital stock. The two effects of such regulations are that the

---

[3] Others have developed comparable notions. Blaikie and Brookfield (1987) for instance, define works such as stone walls, terraces, field drains, irrigation systems, drainage and reclamation systems as capital, because the life of these investments exceeds that of the crop or crop cycle. Coward's insight elaborates this concept for understanding water distribution processes on irrigation schemes and for improving the effectiveness of public assistance to irrigation development.

ownership of and responsibility for the irrigation works invariably coincide, and that the social relationships between the members of the water board, the water guards and the water users are not based on kinship or some obscure form of ethnic homogeneity but on ownership of the hydraulic property.

The concept of irrigation development as a process of property creation is an ideal or abstraction. It identifies the relationships that structure many cases of irrigation development, without describing any concrete case. The concept does not describe any concrete case of irrigation development, as property relationships are everywhere tied up with ecological, historical, legislative, economic and other specifics. The use of the notion lies in its power to help understand water distribution processes.

Outsiders to the irrigation development scene may easily underestimate the value of the concept. They do not know that the notion of property used to be outside the frame of reference of most irrigation experts. An example of this frame of reference may be found in this collection of case studies. In Chapter 4, Gerbrandy and Hoogendam describe experienced engineers working on a system in Bolivia. Only after a series of sometimes violent clashes with the farmers did the project team realize that water was distributed in terms of rights. And even then the team members did not recognize these rights as shares in property.

We ourselves had a similar experience in a research project on water management in the Senegal river valley. The social equality between farmers on the 20 ha village schemes was wholly at odds with the social inequality reigning in the villages between freeborn and the descendants of slaves. In the traditional system in the villages, the descendants of slaves could not own agricultural land, participate in village politics, ride a horse, own a cart or marry a freeborn partner. Many lived in separate, crowded wards. But on the new irrigation schemes, plots were of equal size and farmers distributed water on the basis of a right that could be expressed as follows: when a person had his turn, he could take as much as he wanted. Only when the field research had been completed and the project had access to the concept of hydraulic property was it realized that the equal size of the plots and the equality in the water rights was probably due to the construction process: freeborn farmers and people of slave descent had made identical investments.[4]

---

[4] Coward himself uses the concept to compare the merits of conventional direct public investment in irrigation with indirect methods such as providing loans to farmers and giving them tax rebates for newly irrigated land. These indirect policies favour farmer ownership of the infrastructure and may help avoid farmers requesting the state to maintain the canals and weirs. In the light of the Senegal experience it may be added that the concept also illustrates the potential for promoting marginalized groups. These may be offered opportunities to invest their labour (or capital that they have been loaned on favourable terms).

Institutional constraints to knowledge of water distribution

An outsider to the irrigation scene in developing countries will be surprised by the lack of a clear overview of the key process of water distribution on schemes that may number up to tens of thousands of farmers. It is not that the water distribution process defies study, as pioneering studies published since 1986 have demonstrated. Rather, the reasons lie in the context in which irrigation engineers operate. For several decades neither their academic nor their institutional environments valued research on or knowledge of the management process.

At many technical universities and institutes, irrigation engineering is a mere subsection of a civil engineering department. The subsection usually teaches irrigation as one of the many fields to which civil engineering may be applied. If the subsection has a research tradition and a research programme (in Europe this was rare before 1985) topics usually involve one of the physical and technical disciplines that make up irrigation engineering: civil engineering, hydrology, soil science, agronomy, hydraulics or a combination of these.

In such an academic context, it is hard to formulate and defend research programmes that focus on issues requiring an input from the behavioural sciences. In cases where in spite of the odds the contact has been established, issues of professional orientation arise. Social scientists are trained in analysis and usually shrink from making predictions, whereas irrigation engineers are design-oriented and look for prescriptions and methods to tackle practical problems. In addition, social scientists are rarely trained to question technical paradigms. Consequently, they rarely question the received professional wisdom of their engineering colleagues.

The institutional contexts of scheme development and scheme management do not encourage irrigation engineers to acquire or disseminate knowledge on actual distribution practices either. Foreign engineers are usually contracted by donor agencies to produce designs for new schemes or to supervise construction. They are rarely involved in the management of their schemes and so cannot incorporate feedback on the distribution practices into their design methods and their assumptions about management.

This lack of feedback has led to many schemes, especially those in sub-Saharan Africa, deteriorating quickly and needing rehabilitation after only a few years. In theory, such rehabilitations provide an opportunity to take into account the management patterns of operators and irrigators. In practice, however, these rehabilitations simply re-establish the physical configuration of the original system.

For a deeper understanding of technical assistance in irrigation one needs to look beyond the engineers to the donor agencies that manage the public development funds and to the national departments of planning, agriculture or water that set objectives for agricultural development. Together, these institutions define the terms of reference that the irrigation engineers are contracted to implement. Almost invariably, these bureaucracies are the initiators of the large schemes. With the help of projections of food requirements based on population growth and changing diets or of demand for a particular commodity, national agricultural production goals are set for rice, wheat, sugar cane, cotton or some other crop. Sites are identified that have physical potential for irrigation. The departments solicit donor help to finance, design and construct the scheme. After conclusive feasibility studies, calculations of the possible internal rates of return of various design options, and negotiations on funding, the donor agency allocates the millions of dollars requested.

This is the process that transpires, as indicated by project documents, but other processes are at work too. Management specialist and irrigation engineer Nijman (1993) has studied the links between donor agencies, national governments and irrigation agencies, and their connections with their environments, with the aim of identifying causes of the annual loss of billions of dollars in the irrigation subsector. Several points stand out from his analysis of eight cases.

The first is that development banks and other donor agencies have so much public capital at their disposal that is earmarked for investment in 'developing' countries that their officers have difficulty finding sufficient 'outlets' and are under constant pressure to maximize loans and grants. This pressure often adversely affects the quality of the investment decisions; real-life feasibility and functionality of the investments, as opposed to the feasibility and functionality assumed in the design reports, are not assessed, performance achievements of the agency and of similar schemes are ignored, and even the water resources available are assessed in an unprofessional manner.

Nijman's second finding concerns the primacy of politics. The governments of most donor countries pursue their own political, as opposed to developmental, objectives in selecting recipient countries, and most national governments pursue their own internal political goals. Investment appraisal techniques such as the economic internal rate of return, cost-benefit analyses and related sensitivity analyses did not render any of the cases studied by Nijman unfeasible as these studies were done after the political decision had been taken to construct a scheme at a certain site. The studies were used to justify the subsidies for irrigation, not to improve economic decision-making.

The fact that development banks are under pressure to transfer public funds to developing countries, plus the fact that much irrigation investment is politically motivated, have instilled an attitude of rent-seeking in the national irrigation agencies. The legal rents consist of charges such as payment of overhead costs to the irrigation agency, investment-related loan payments for new buildings, machinery, vehicles, training courses and daily allowances, and a reduction of the funds allocated to maintenance. The illegal rents consist of bribes. Nijman cites sources that say that 30 to 70 per cent of construction funds are 'leaked' in Sri Lanka, 58 per cent in Pakistan and 50 per cent in India.

Often the irrigation investments also contribute to the desire of the national elite to 'modernize' the countryside and its inhabitants. Examples are the expensive Kano and Bakolori schemes in northern Nigeria (Adams 1992). Irrigation schemes may also be part of a policy to keep rural populations where they are, as Konings (1986) has demonstrated for the Vea and Tono schemes in northern Ghana, or to lessen population pressure in areas where the elite holds much land by creating new settler areas, as Dunham (1983) has demonstrated for the Mahaweli scheme in Sri Lanka.

Management of the schemes is usually a matter for national engineers employed by the national irrigation agencies. Because the funding of most agencies does not depend on their performance in water delivery, most national engineers have little incentive to entangle with farmers, colleagues and politicians to improve water delivery. These engineers do of course intimately know the day-to-day water distribution, but refrain from publishing their insights for at least two reasons. The first is that actual operation usually deviates from the assumptions in the design. A detailed description of these deviations might lead to the national engineers being accused of incompetence. The second reason is that political patronage and corruption are endemic in many schemes because they form part of the national political landscape. A description of actual as opposed to planned allocations would expose these practices on which the publishing engineer himself depends for his livelihood. (See Wade 1988 and the observations in the contribution by Mollinga and Bolding in Chapter 2 of this volume.)

The global institutional picture and this collection of papers

Present academic and institutional contexts do not offer irrigation engineers many incentives to improve systematic knowledge of the distribution of irrigation water as a process between people on the one hand and between people and objects on the other. The academic context favours only the elaboration of knowledge of distribution as a process between artifacts; plants, structures, canals, fields. It has discouraged forms of collaboration between irrigation engineering and the type of qualitative social science that is required.

The work environment offers substantial rewards for ignorance of actual distribution processes and few rewards for the development and diffusion of systematic knowledge. Foreign engineers rarely manage the schemes that they design, and consequently can rarely verify their assumptions. Engineers contracted to produce a feasibility report will hesitate to describe a proposal as unfeasible because they risk losing later contracts, either for the design and implementation of the proposal or for the assessment of new proposals. For reasons of budget, career or international relations, donor officials are unwilling to slow down the identification, assessment, approval and implementation of investment opportunities while awaiting the results of studies or negotiations with operators and farmers.

To the national irrigation agency or ministry, irrigation infrastructures are powerful tools for modernizing agriculture and rural society. Since the agency or ministry owns the canals, and sometimes also the land, its engineers consider that they can direct agricultural production towards modern crops and national objectives. In their view it is only logical to exclude the supposedly ignorant and tradition-bound farmers from water management and to design smallholder schemes as if they are the property of a single farm, on which water is distributed by a central manager. National engineers who question the feasibility of this run the risk of being accused of betraying the modernizing, if not civilizing, mission of the national government, even if they base their objections on the outcome of prior schemes.

National engineers work for irrigation agencies, either directly or through consulting firms. Their bosses and they themselves depend for part of their income on the rents that spin off from donor disbursements. This dependence encourages them to accept any donor wishes regarding water distribution, whether effective or inappropriate, and makes them reluctant to make comments that might cause the donor to reconsider the investment proposal.

The professional context explains why irrigation engineers know little about actual distribution processes. When they are designers it is sufficient, and even more beneficial to them, to accept current assumptions about the cultivator and his crops, to see farmers as a group and to accept the need for central management of the schemes, because these assumptions fit the goals of the donor agency and the recipient government. Designers are practically constrained to embrace these assumptions, because in reality there are only about ten potential clients. The designers' interests lie in maintaining the status quo as the other clients would sooner or later learn of any dissent. Hence designers share these assumptions, even when from experience they know them to be illusory, since they do not stem from empirical research. (See also Nijman 1993.) To engineers who are managers, any systematic description of actual processes will lead to trouble with their colleagues (who may feel compromised), fear that the donor will hesitate to make new investments, or both.

If the distribution of water is not only a physical but also a social process, evaluations of the operation of irrigation systems are also evaluations of the distribution of rights and obligations between the parties. In the case of public irrigation this means evaluating the distribution of rights and obligations between the agency and the farmers; in the case of public intervention in farmer-managed irrigation it means recognizing existing rights. In other words, the analysis and improvement of water distribution processes involves the analysis, and probably reform, of property relationships and entitlements. This is of course a sensitive issue where national governments claim ownership of land and/or water and wish to constrain the farmers to grow the crops selected in the national plan. Such evaluations require political will and analytical insight. This book aims at contributing to insight in the hope of reinforcing the political will.

The book opens with a case study by Mollinga and Bolding about the social construction of outlets on a large irrigation scheme in South India. They discuss variations in the construction of the pipe outlets that are supposed to be standard, and relate the differences and deviations to interaction, including struggle, between farmers and the Irrigation Department. The four contributions that follow (Chapters 3–6) compare the conventional engineering viewpoints on water management with distribution practices on farmer-managed schemes. The comparisons are made within the framework of public efforts to 'rehabilitate' or 'improve' some farmer-managed schemes. Since site, climate and crops are kept constant, the case studies reveal the impact of institutions on the views of engineers and farmers about the distribution of water. In each, attention is given to division structures and canals as the tangible result of views on how irrigation water should be managed.

Chapter 7, by Hoogendam, Van den Dries, Portela, Stam and Carvalho, studies a different topic: the rules for transforming the allocation of water into actual distribution. The collection ends with two chapters that study policies to mobilize farmer-managed irrigation for national production objectives. Van den Dries, Hoogendam and Portela (Chapter 8) compare four principles of water allocation encountered on farmer-managed schemes in Portugal, taking as their starting point an EU programme to improve the yield of livestock. They study the leeway that these principles give farmers to irrigate meadows with the additional irrigation water resulting from an improvement programme. Dia, Diemer, Van Driel and Huibers (Chapter 9) report on an experiment in the Senegal river valley. As a team of social scientists and irrigation engineers they attempted to apply farmer management practices which were successful on 20 ha schemes to the design of a 400 ha scheme.

2. Signposts of struggle

Pipe outlets as the material interface between water users and the state in a large-scale irrigation system in South India[1]

PETER P. MOLLINGA and ALEX BOLDING

Large-scale irrigation systems in India are jointly managed. Both the farmers/water users and the government are involved in water distribution and in the maintenance of the irrigation system. The Irrigation Department of the government is responsible for management tasks 'above the outlet', whereas farmers are responsible for 'below the outlet'. The physical link between these two domains is the outlet structure to the tertiary unit.[2] Through the outlet the Irrigation Department supplies certain amounts of water to groups of farmers, who then distribute this water among themselves.[3] This paper examines the connection between these two domains in a large-scale canal system in South India,[4] to ascertain what happens at this interface.

It is well known that farmers generally do not sit and wait to see how much water the Irrigation Department will supply, and when it prefers to do

---

[1] The research on which this chapter is based was financially supported by WOTRO (Netherlands Foundation for the Advancement of Tropical Research), which is gratefully acknowledged.

[2] The tertiary unit is referred to in North India as *chak*, meaning delimited area, in South India as outlet *ayacut* (or *atchkat*), which means the area commanded by the outlet.

[3] Contrary to what is often assumed, the legal definitions of responsibilities and domains are different. For example in Karnataka, one of the South Indian States, cultivators are indeed legally obliged to maintain field channels 'below the outlet'. But regarding the distribution of water, the Karnataka Irrigation Rules (1965) state 'water shall not be drawn from the field channel except from the points fixed by the Irrigation Officer' and 'the order in which water shall be supplied to the different lands from the field channel shall be determined by the Irrigation Officer'. We know of no effort in Karnataka where the Irrigation Department has tried to intervene in water management 'below the outlet' so directly. Command Area Development Authorities were established between 1974 and 1980 to be responsible 'for water utilisation and integrated area development in the irrigation command, including modernisation of the distribution system, the provision of drainage and the maintenance and operation of both the distribution and drainage systems.' (Setting up of CAD Authorities notification of 1.9.73). The attempt to introduce *warabandi*, a form of rotational water supply, in the South Indian systems is an unsuccessful attempt by the Command Area Development Authorities, not by the Irrigation Department, to intervene in management 'below the outlet'. The main system domain is itself contested within the administration although the Irrigation Department has effectively claimed that main system management is its exclusive domain. See Chambers (1988: 88–89) for further discussion.

[4] The command area of the system is 240 000 ha, the length of the main canal 227 km, with a design discharge of 4100 cusecs (116 m³/s). From the main canal 87 secondary canals called distributaries take off, which supply water to thousands of outlets, directly from the distributary or via sub-distributaries. The design discharge of the outlet structure is generally 1 cusec (28.3 l/s).

so, but that they actively intervene in the management 'above the outlet', to secure sufficient water supply to their fields (Chambers, 1988). This means that the outlet structure is a site of struggle between farmers/water users and the Irrigation Department, rather than the locus of transfer of respon-sibilities.

In interior South India, the large-scale systems are so-called protective irrigation systems. These systems aim to spread water thinly over a large area and a large number of farmers, in order to protect crops against drought and farmers against famine. The target crops (food crops such as sorghum and millets and cash crops such as oilseeds and cotton) do not require much water. This cropping pattern of 'dry' crops has been enforced by law in the 'localization' system − a form of land use planning which prescribes which crops farmers are allowed, and not allowed, to grow.[5] In practice, however, farmers are not content to grow these 'dry' crops but want to grow 'wet' crops like rice and sugar-cane, which are much more remunerative and require more water. Farmers whose fields are located favourably at the head ends of canals appropriate more water than their legal entitlement, to grow these 'wet' crops, to the detriment of tail end farmers, who get very little or no water at all as a result. Thus the typical problem of unequal water distribution among head end and tail end sections of the system emerges.[6]

This inequitable water distribution is produced and reproduced every day, in sometimes fierce and spectacular interaction between farmers and the Irrigation Department engineers responsible for canal management. This paper seeks to demonstrate that this interaction is not only a social process among people, but also has a material component. The outlet structures are not just the *site* of interaction but also its *subject*. The technical characteristics of the outlet structures constrain social inter-action and are themselves shaped and reshaped by it. The design and construction characteristics of the outlet structures can be understood as the expression of the balance of forces between farmers and the Irrigation Department engineers, a material result of their relationship, which in turn conditions further interaction between the two groups. The first two simple case studies illustrate that outlet structures are signposts of the struggle between farmers and Irrigation Department engineers over the distribution of water.

---

[5] For further discussion of the concept of protective irrigation, see Mollinga 1992.
[6] Implicit here is a simple geographical concept of heads and tails, based on proximity to and distance from the water source. There is a strong correlation between access to water and location along the canal, but more factors do play a role. A discussion of these factors is beyond the scope of this paper.

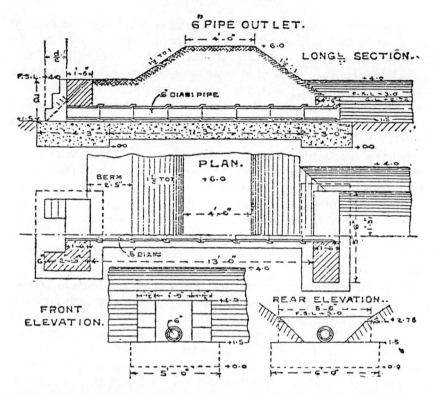

Figure 1 *Pipe outlet of glazed earthenware pipes without gate structure (Source: Ellis, 1931: 304)*

Signposts

In South India, the tertiary unit is usually connected to the main system by a pipe outlet. The origins of the pipe outlet are not clear. Pipe outlets were used in the delta systems of Madras Presidency from the 19th century, and were adopted in the protective irrigation systems of interior South India and the Deccan Plateau. One such scheme is the subject of this paper.[7]

[7] The North Indian and Bombay Presidency outlets have a more spectacular history than the South Indian ones (see Mahbub and Gulhati 1951; Bolding, Mollinga and van Straaten 1995). In South India the pipe outlet is still the dominant structure. Only in the context of World Bank projects (for example the Upper Krishna Project) and programmes (for example the National Water Management Project) are other structures now being introduced. It is unclear why technological dependence on the pipe outlet was so consistent when knowledge was available about other types of outlets (MERS 1966). An advantage of pipe outlets is that they require low 'driving heads' (see below). This partly explains their popularity in the flat delta areas, where little head is available. In interior South India however, sufficient head is available, because of the undulating topography, to allow the use of other structures.

A pipe outlet is exactly what its name implies. It is a pipe under one of the canal banks which lets water out of the distribution canal into the subsidiary canal of the outlet *ayacut*, that is, the network of field channels. A pipe outlet structure need be no more than an open pipe through a canal bank. The standard design is, however, somewhat more elaborate. It includes a head and an end wall on the upstream and the downstream sides, in which the pipe is fixed (see Figure 1 for an early example, used in Madras Presidency).

Hydraulically, pipe outlets are non-modular structures, that is, the discharge through the pipe depends on both the upstream and the downstream canal water level. Discharge further depends on the pipe cross section.[8] The difference between the upstream and downstream water levels is the 'driving head' of the outlet.[9] Nowadays, the pipes are mostly round, concrete pipes (Hume pipes), placed horizontally at canal bed level.[10] On the upstream side there is generally a closing mechanism: a steel or wooden gate.

The protective irrigation systems of South India are designed as continuous flow systems, with constant discharge over the cropping season. The outlet's dimensions are calculated on the basis of the size of the outlet *ayacut* and its 'localized' cropping pattern, and the design characteristics (full supply water levels) of the upstream and downstream canals. The gates provided, mostly sliding steel gates on the upstream side, were originally not intended to regulate the flow, but only to be opened or closed (on or off). The pipe outlet structure design is based on a low intensity management structure in a supply-oriented system with continuous flow and constant discharge.

The need to ration water is built into the system because a protective irrigation system aims to spread water thinly. This mode of water distribution requires farmers to allow water to flow past their fields to benefit others, even though they could very well use the water themselves. This proposition became very contentious after the advent of the Green Revolution. High-yielding varieties of remunerative crops such as rice required much more water than sorghum and millets. Also, the importance of timing the water supply grew, as these varieties were very sensitive to water stress. Pipe outlets were not designed for 'fine tuning' and coping with varying

---

[8] Except of course when there is free outfall on the downstream side of the pipe. But this is not how the pipe outlets are normally designed.

[9] The general formula for discharge of pipe outlets, $Q = C_d.A.(2gH)^{\frac{1}{2}}$, in which C_d is the discharge coefficient of the outlet, A the area of the pipe opening, and H the driving head.

[10] When pipe outlets draw water from deep canals, the pipe may be located not at the canal bed but higher. In interior South India, where most systems are reservoir systems, canal water does not have a large silt load. This load is therefore not a design consideration, in contrast to the North Indian river diversion systems that tap water from the Himalayan rivers.

demands. Farmers had to interfere with the outlet structure to get the amount of water they wanted at the time they needed it.

There are at least two ways in which farmers can manipulate the structure in order to increase the discharge through the pipe. One is increasing the driving head, by raising the upstream water level (for example, by blocking the canal with stones or bathing buffaloes) or lowering the downstream water level (for example, by digging out the canal bed when sufficient head is available). Another strategy is to increase the pipe's cross-section, by convincing the Irrigation Department to install a larger pipe, by damaging the pipe and creating favourable leakages, or by installing an extra, illegal, pipe.

The general response of the Irrigation Department to these interventions of the farmers has been to start using the gate of the pipe outlet to regulate the water flow, by making the gate adjustable, and putting a lock on it. In this way, the Irrigation Department has tried to control the flow through the outlets and to fulfil its responsibility of distributing water equitably among all farmers.[11]

The increase in demand for water has led to the pipe outlet becoming the site of interaction between farmers and Irrigation Department officials regarding discharges flowing through it. In this process the outlets themselves have been modified. The type of modification, and the resulting characteristics of the outlet structure depend on the scarceness of water and the modes of interaction (and their development over time) of the groups of people involved. Hence, the characteristics of outlet structures will differ from place to place in the system; for example, along a distributary canal. In this section we give two examples of this spatial differentiation, and suggest its social significance.[12]

---

[11] The regulation of water flow by partial closure of the pipe opening is not a fully quantitative regulation. To establish the discharge in l/s or cusecs, one would have to measure the upstream water level, the pipe opening/gate level, and the downstream water level, and calculate the discharge with the discharge formula. As the protective systems have no cross-regulating structures in the canals, water levels change frequently, such as when farmers manipulate outlets or change downstream water levels, for example by 'heading up' the canal water level to irrigate high-lying plots. A constant discharge into the outlet *ayacut* would require very frequent adjustment of the gate level; this does not happen. Instead, a required average gate opening is calculated, expressed in a number of threads or inches, and it is attempted to keep to this. Even though this gate opening is the subject of negotiation between ID (Irrigation Department) officials and farmers, it is a management tool for the ID. The effort to regulate flows by gate settings stimulated farmers to seek new strategies to increase supply: convincing ID officials to raise the gates, or manipulating the gates themselves.

[12] The order of presentation is the reverse of the order of discovery. In the field research underlying this chapter, we first empirically found differences in the design and construction of pipe outlets and only subsequently were able to explain these by examining the processes of social interaction connected to them.

From head to tail in a sub-distributary

The first example is a sub-distributary at the tail end of a head end distributary. This distributary, being in the head end of the system, was constructed in the early stages of the project more than 35 years ago.[13] As a result of this long period, a head–tail distribution of water has crystallized, closely fitting the geographical pattern of proximity to or distance from the water source.[14] This is also clear in the sub-distributary canal discussed here. In almost 3 km the situation changes from 100 per cent rice cultivation in two seasons in the first outlet *ayacuts*, to less than 10 per cent rice cultivation in one season in one of the last outlet *ayacuts*. This change is also visible in the pipe outlet structures. The sub-distributary can be divided into four sections. In each of the sections we find a different type of pipe outlet, related to a different water management situation.

In 35 years of water distribution the outlets of the sub-distributary have undergone several changes as a result of increasing water scarcity. At the very beginning, when as yet there was no water scarcity, pipes of standard size were installed in the outlets of this sub-distributary, with 'pen-gates'. These gates could be fixed at different levels by inserting a wooden or iron 'pen', or rather pin, through the holes made at regular intervals in the handle of the shutter. This gate type is now distant history, and most farmers only know the thread-gates that are presently used (see Photograph 1). In the thread-gate the gate handle is a long bolt, and a hexagonal nut has to be turned with a special key to raise or lower it. The mechanism also has a spring lock, for which an additional key is needed. The thread-gates were introduced when water distribution problems started occurring, and the gates began to be used as regulating and control devices to limit discharges into the outlets. But thread-gates can also be manipulated by farmers, either by damaging them or by copying the keys. In the 1980s, with increasing water scarcity, another change took place. The Irrigation Department adjusted (in effect, reduced) the standard size pipes to diameters calculated on the basis of the command areas of the outlets. This is what all outlet structures of the sub-distributary have in common: thread-gates and redesigned pipe diameters.

The details of the shape of the outlet structures vary from head to tail. In the first, head end section of the sub-distributary the problem is excessive

---

[13] The command area of this distributary is 7493 ha, of the sub-distributary it is 520 ha.
[14] In this distributary the land 'localized' for 'wet' crops (rice and sugarcane) was located in the low-lying tail end areas, and these were the areas first developed by farmers for irrigation. Initially therefore, the water head was located in the geographical tail. In the course of time a reversal of head and tail took place as a result of land development in all parts of the distributary command and because of the disregard of the 'localization' pattern by cultivators. As a result the tail end sub-distributary discussed here, which is fully 'localized' for sugarcane cultivation, started suffering from water shortage.

Photograph 1 *Thread-gate mechanism found on the canal side (held by research assistant R. Doraiswamy)*

withdrawal of water for the cultivation of two crops of rice per year. In an effort to control damage to the gate/outlet structure and prevent manipulation, the Irrigation Department has constructed what can best be called 'bunkers' at the first six outlets (1, 2 and 3, left side and right side, Figure

Photograph 2 *The bunker type outlet*

2). These are heavy, rectangular concrete blocks of about 0.8×1.6 m^2, with the gate mechanism in the middle of the concrete block, hidden and protected in the structure (see Photograph 2). The gate itself is concealed, and cannot easily be reached by hand, hammer or crowbar. The lock mechanism is – necessarily – visible and can be reached on the outside top; it remains the Achilles heel of the structure. However, as it is less easy to inflict physical damage on this structure than on other types, it is mostly manipulated by means of copied keys. The relation between the farmers and the Irrigation Department operators is now one of negotiating the number of threads that the gate is opened.

The second, middle section of the sub-distributary consists of eight outlets of a different construction (4, 5, 6 and 7, left side and right side, Figure 2). They are built of local granite and mortar, the original materials used in all structures. The gates are visible and accessible (Photograph 3, page 20). The structures are smaller than the 'bunkers' in the first canal section. Many of the middle section outlets have been slightly damaged to increase the discharge through the pipe – for example, by cutting a hole in the structure, so that when the water level is higher than the gate, water can also enter the pipe over the gate rather than under it. Apart from manipulating the gates themselves, the farmers in this section of the canal try to raise water levels in the sub-distributary by creating obstructions from stones, wood, mud and straw. This is possible in this canal section because

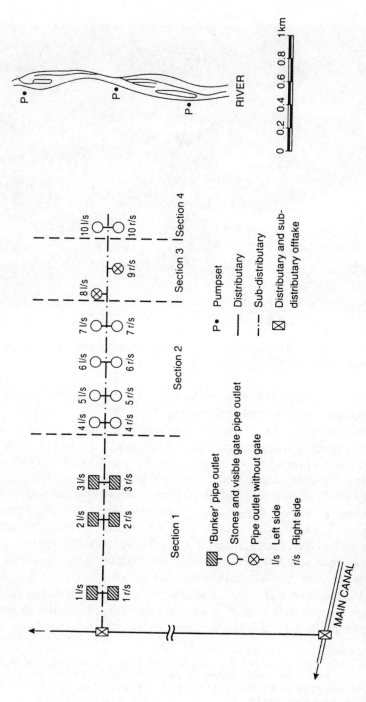

Figure 2 *Spatial distribution of different types of pipe outlet structures along a sub-distributary*

Photograph 3 *The stone-and-mortar type outlet with a visible gate (with canal obstruction)*

water levels are lower than in the first section. There the canal is still so deep and wide that obstruction is not easy.

In the third section of the sub-distributary the situation is different again. Here, water is really scarce. Outlet 8 left side is a structure of the stones and visible gate type, but the gate is no longer there. When this pipe was scheduled to be changed from a 1 foot diameter pipe to a smaller pipe, the farmers fiercely protested.[15] The farmers allege that an official verbally abused a leading farmer during one discussion between farmers and Irrigation Department officials. The farmer then gripped the official by his collar. As a 'punishment', the official installed the smallest available pipe – one with a 6 inch diameter – after which the farmers removed the gate mechanism. The situation was left at that.

Pipe outlet 9 right side consists solely of a pipe under the canal bank, with a small wall built of stones on the canal side. A full structure was never built, even though the gate mechanism was brought to the site.

---

[15] And with some reason. The calculation of the pipe diameter is based on the design water level in the sub-distributary but this level is never reached in the tail because the upstream pipe outlets draw off excess water. For further discussion of pipe outlet design calculations, see footnote 25.

According to the Irrigation Department canal operators, it was not built because the closure period of the canal ended before construction could start. It is more likely that the structure is absent because the outlet is opposite the house of a local political leader, whose family and clients have land in this *ayacut*, and who is an important liaison person for the Irrigation Department.[16] Both the 8 left side and 9 right side outlets are 'operated' by putting obstructions in the canal, and, more importantly, by guarding upstream sections and gates (removing obstructions, etc.).

In the fourth section, the pipe outlet structures are again of the stones and visible gate type, and they are in good condition (10 left side and right side, Figure 2). The reason is that hardly any water reaches this point. The height of the gate opening is of no consequence, as water levels hardly ever exceed one or two inches. Also, the commands of these two outlets are largely irrigated through pump-lift irrigation from the river, and waste water drawn from a drain. Farmers have solved the scarcity problem by tapping other water sources. Thus in the fourth as well as in the third section of the sub-distributary, the pipe outlets are no more than pipes, and their technical state is quite irrelevant, as the main problem is getting water to these sections in the first place.

The example of this sub-distributary shows that the condition and characteristics of pipe outlet structures cannot be understood simply in terms of the quality of maintenance, or technical/constructive sophistication. This condition and these characteristics are related to the mode of water distribution and the connected social interaction between water users and Irrigation Department officials.

Migrant entrepreneurs in a tail end distributary

The second example of spatial differentiation in outlet structure characteristics is situated in a tail end distributary. An important aspect of this case is the effect of settlement of migrant farmers on water distribution.

The construction of this irrigation system attracted many outside farmers, who migrated from the delta region of a neighbouring state, where land prices and the pressure on the land were high. These farmers could sell for high prices in their home areas and buy cheaply in the new system. Apart from investment capital, the settlers brought highly developed agronomic and entrepreneurial skills to an area which was poor and had low levels of productivity. The settler farmers acquired land in favourable locations along the canals, and established highly productive but water-intensive rice-based farming systems. The settler farmers became the first head enders. In the older distributaries, sections of the original population

---

[16] For example, through this person the Irrigation Department recruits and pays extra canal operators to guard the canal at night during crisis periods.

have followed suit, but in the newer distributaries, such as the one discussed in this example, this is less pronounced.[17]

The settlement of migrant farmers also accelerated change on this canal. The medium-sized distributary (command area 4687 ha) in the tail end area of the main canal discussed here, has been operational since approximately 1968. But only after about 1978 did migrant farmers start to settle along this canal. As a result, in 1992 the mode of water distribution was still in flux. Up to 1980, little land had been developed for irrigation and the land which had been developed was almost exclusively for 'dry' crops like sorghum, millet and cotton. Between 1978 and 1990 the rice area increased from several tens of hectares to 1500 ha, most of which is cultivated by settler farmers. The demand for water in the distributary increased enormously, and the canal changed from a no-problem to a problem case. There is now considerable conflict over water distribution in the distributary. For reasons explained below, the migrant farmers settled in the middle reach.[18] Rice cultivation has increased so much that now the tail end section of the distributary often receives water that is insufficient even for the 'dry' crops.

As in the previous example, the pipe outlet structures were originally built of granite and mortar, and furnished with pen-gates. The pen-gates, replaced with thread-gates, can still be found in the area, even if all that survives is a post for tethering buffaloes. The problem caused by increased water scarcity led to the destruction of most pipe outlet structures: gates were removed, and half or more of the stonework was demolished in some cases (see Photographs 4 and 5). The response of the Irrigation Department has been to start constructing more solid, concrete structures in the place of the stone-and-mortar ones.[19] The spread of these new structures in 1991–2 illustrates the water management problems in this distributary (see Figure 3).

The migrant farmers settled on the banks of the canal, in or near the fields they cultivate. From Figure 3 it is clear that the Irrigation Department started its work of reconstructing the pipe outlet structures in the area close to the migrant settlements (called 'camps') and that the settlers dominate the middle section of the canal. The other sections, closer to the original villages, take their water through the original stone-and-mortar structures. In the head end there is no great need for water control, as water use is low.

---

[17] A complex process is crudely summarized here. It is one thing that the settler farmers acted as 'inducers of innovation' but another how the local population did or did not respond to this. The slow and hesitant reaction of local farmers to the modernizing force of irrigation and the settlers is connected with the nature of the rainfed farming system and farmers' perceptions of soil quality, with skill and experience, with oppressive social relations and with indebtedness. Discussion of this complexity is beyond the scope of this book.

[18] This is thus a case where the head in terms of water distribution is not the geographical head of the canal.

[19] These are of the visible gate type. The bunker type still has to be introduced.

Photograph 4 *Half demolished stone-and-mortar pipe outlet with gate frame still visible*

Photograph 5 *Demolished stone-and-mortar pipe outlet with raised gate mechanism*

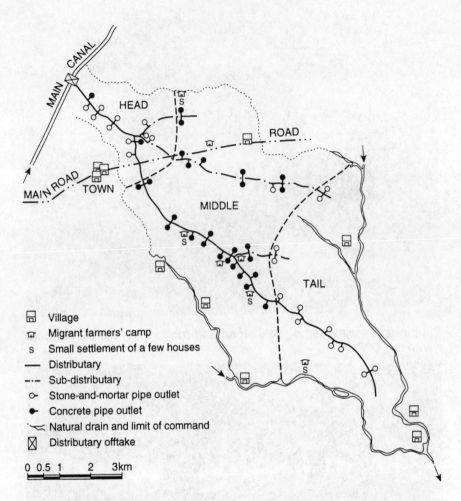

Figure 3 *Spatial distribution of different types of pipe outlet structures along a distributary*

The landlords from the local town own most of the land and refuse to sell it to settler farmers. They have only recently started to develop their land for intensive irrigated agriculture.[20] As in the previous example, in the tail end section of the distributary the problem is not the condition of the pipe outlet structures, but the arrival of water.

The tail end villages are dominated by a few landlords who are also moneylenders and employers. This hampers locally organized pressure

---

[20] This land is often levelled and equipped with bunds and field channels by settler farmers to whom the land has been leased for a period of three to seven years.

being put on the middle-reach farmers and on the Irrigation Department to supply more water. For many inhabitants the benefits of extra supplies are small because the trickle-down effect of these supplies is generally poor. As a result, the middle-reach farmers have so far been able to appropriate water in quantities sufficient for themselves. During the daytime the Irrigation Department lowers the middle-reach gates so that some water goes to the tail end section. Outside working hours, the canal and the gates are the domain of the middle-reach farmers, who raise the gates with duplicate keys.[21] A compromise has been struck, similar to that reached in the case of the first six outlets of the sub-distributary discussed above; however, here the farmers are in a stronger position.

Both the sub-distributary and the distributary case exemplify the significance of the material characteristics of pipe outlet structures for the social dynamics of water distribution. If nothing else, these structures are signposts of complex social processes. The two cases also suggest that the shape of each structure is itself the subject of negotiation and change. This point is elaborated in the following section, where we focus on the *process* of negotiating and renegotiating the shape of pipe outlets.

Struggle

Our next case history is a story about a distributary at the tail end of the main canal. Water has become scarce over the years and this growing scarcity has led to fierce interaction on the canals and elsewhere. The confrontation between the Irrigation Department officials and farmers over water distribution has triggered a process of redesigning the pipe outlet structures. This process went through several phases, described below, in which different types of pipe outlet structures emerged. Since there is a continuous need to repair damaged pipe outlet structures, there is always an opportunity to replace them with new types. As this damage is not spread uniformly along the canal (see Table 1), different types of pipe outlets can be found in different places. A discussion of the spatial distribution of these types would take too long, because this distributary has a complex history and a large command area (12 932 ha). We concentrate on the evolution of the design of the pipe outlet structure over time.

Phase 1: the 1960s and 1970s
The construction of the 16 km long distributary was completed in 1964. Initially, local cultivators were somewhat reluctant to develop their land

---

[21] Since 1980 the Irrigation Department has followed several strategies to curb water use in the middle reach, including a 'law and order' campaign and the introduction of rotation over canal sections.

Table 1: Number and percentage of damaged pipe outlets on the main distributary as a function of relative distance from distributary intake

Rank number (from head to tail)	Number damaged	Percentage damaged
1–15	15	100
16–30	12	80
31–46	6	37.5

and to start practising irrigated agriculture.[22] This indicates that there was ample water at the time. In view of the abundance of the supply compared with demand, the distributary was extended in 1969 to a total length of 31 km.[23] Approximately 100 pipe outlets now tap water from the distributary and its sub-distributaries.

With the immigration of settler farmers, demand for irrigation water rose gradually, as they cultivated rice and developed large pieces of land. In the 1970s patches of land must have been developed all along the canal. In the tail end village of the canal – Km 30–31 is a common way of expressing this (30–31 km along the distributary from the offtake point) – groundnuts were grown under irrigation on the fertile red soils that occur here. In the head reaches of the distributary and sub-distributaries, settlers grew rice. The local landlords sold most of what is now head end land to the settlers. They wished to keep their land near the villages, not realizing that these lands would later become tail end locations.[24]

During this period we find pen-gates without padlocks. On the sub-distributaries the steel gates of the pipe outlet structures were cast in a vertical round pipe, as pipes were readily available during the construction of the canal system. The pipe outlets on the distributary itself were of a more fortified type, with the pen-gate cast in a U-shaped concrete block (see Photographs 6 and 7).

The pipe diameters were systematically designed larger than required, given the localization pattern and the maximum water levels in the

---

[22] For the phenomenon of unwanted water in protective irrigation, see Attwood (1987). For a field report from the early days of the irrigation system discussed here, see Nair (1961: 46–51).

[23] This extension was an electoral promise of a local parliamentary candidate.

[24] The original villages are located in the low parts of the area near the natural drains, as this was where drinking water could be found longest in the past, and where the soils were most suitable for cultivation as they held more water than the soils in the higher parts (infiltrated run-off). The canals were constructed on the highest parts, the ridges, where the migrants also built their 'camps'. With the advent of irrigation the spatial pattern of water availability was reversed.

Photograph 6 *The vertical pipe type outlet*

Photograph 7 *Outlet with a concrete U-shaped block, with pen-gate or thread-gate*

canals.[25] The management of the pipe outlets by the Irrigation Department
was of low intensity. Each gangman, the unskilled Irrigation Department
employee responsible for operating gates, oversaw the operation of three to
four pipe outlets. It was considered unneccessary to have gauge readers to
monitor water levels in the canal. This type of outlet and low surveillance
intensity allowed farmers to appropriate water easily for water-intensive
cropping patterns.

Phase 2: the 1980s to 1987

In this phase the *status quo* between the cultivators and the Irrigation
Department changed and gradually an unmaintainable situation emerged.
More and more land was developed, and the cropping pattern shifted towards
'wet' crops. The Irrigation Department started to face a water distribution
problem, because the water supply remained the same, or even decreased
due to growing demand in the upstream distributaries. Average daily
supply in the dry season (December–March) fell over the years, with
1986 as the lowest point. A new type of pipe outlet was introduced in
the sub-distributaries to replace the damaged 'vertical pipe with pen-gate'
type of outlet. The vertical pipe was replaced by a more robust rectangular
block built of granite stones. More gangmen were deployed – one for
every two to three outlets – but the outlets were still easily manipulated.
The tail end of the distributary started to fall dry. At first the water still
reached Km 31, but later it only got as far as Km 28 and Km 25.[26]

In the second half of the 1980s the tail enders organized themselves into
a 'body'.[27] This organization of over 350 water users organized actions
against the Irrigation Department in order to increase the water supply to
the tail end reaches. From 1984 to 1987 this organization was responsible

---

[25] The reasons for designing too large pipes are not clear. In the design routine the
diameter of the pipe is the variable. Engineers explain the routine as determining the
correct pipe diameter for given water levels (driving head) and design discharge of the
outlet. The decision to use larger pipe diameters is subsequently justified in two ways; as
'being on the safe side', as the design data (notably the actual head available) are
inaccurate, and as fear that the pipe will be obstructed if it is too narrow. In later stages
of the system's existence it may also be anticipation of real water levels in tail end
sections of distributaries being lower than full supply depth, the use of the shutter as a
regulating device, and resistance of farmers to pipes of small diameter. Pipes that are too
large and are equipped with gates that regulate the discharge allow ID officials to adjust
the gate to changing demands and pressures. This flexibility is potentially an advantage
over narrow pipes without gates, as it may help to avoid damage and conflicts.

[26] The cut-off point is water reaching the area less than three times per season. Three
irrigations are required for cultivating irrigated sunflower, a popular crop in the command
area.

[27] The organization never had an official name nor any legal status. It was formed
spontaneously during one of the many strikes (*bandhs*) of tail enders at a point halfway
along the distributary. A president, secretary and treasurer were appointed, and every
member had to pay Rs10 per acre as contribution. Besides actions upstream of their pipe

for many violent actions, the operation of pipe outlets and of the intake of the distributary from the main canal, strikes at the offices of the Irrigation Department and physical threats to Irrigation Department officials to obtain more water. The authority of the Irrigation Department crumbled and its power proved to be weak. Police cases were booked against the 'body' but were suspended, thanks to the intervention of local members of parliament (MLAs) and other politicians backing the cultivators. The Revenue department, which collects the penalties imposed by the Irrigation Department to correct farmer behaviour, also proved susceptible to political influence. Practically speaking, the pipe outlets were controlled by the cultivators.

The end of this period was marked by the 'body' being dissolved in 1987. There were several reasons for this break-up. As explained by the original treasurer, there was no longer unity among the farmers. Initially, when one member did not receive sufficient water, a delegation of members would go to the Irrigation Department office, or forcibly raise the gates out of solidarity with that one member. This feeling of solidarity disappeared and people became focused on their own water situation only. Why bother about others some kilometres downstream? It seems likely that water scarcity became so acute that collective organization was no longer feasible (cf. Wade 1987). Another reason is that one Irrigation Department officer working on this canal succeeded in mobilizing sufficient political support to get the 'body' convicted for illegal activities at the district court.[28]

Phase 3: 1987 to 1989

In this period the Irrigation Department tried to regain control over water distribution and concentrated on the control of the operation of the pipe outlets. It designed and constructed a new pipe outlet: the fortified thread-gate. This is the same type of structure as the fortified pen-gate, but with the pen-gate replaced with a thread-gate. The shutter can be moved up and down by turning a hexagonal nut with a special key. This turning mechanism is sometimes covered with a small iron box that can be locked with a padlock. The Irrigation Department thus tried to make it impossible for the farmers to manipulate the gate. Also, in principle, the thread-gate allows the gate opening to be regulated very precisely, whereas the pen-gate had only four to five positions in which it could be fixed. The thread-gates were installed along the main distributary and along the sub-distributary where most members of the collapsed 'body' had their land.

With the same determination to retake charge of the water distribution, the Irrigation Department fortified the intakes of the sub-distributaries. The

---

[28] After this conviction, the officer was demoted to supervise a sub-distributary, whereas previously he had been responsible for a whole section of the distributary. Apparently, this action against the 'body' had triggered other political forces who organized his demotion.

number of staff on the canal was increased. Whereas there had previously been one Assistant Engineer/Section Officer for the whole canal, the distributary was divided into four sections, each with an Assistant Engineer/Section Officer. More gangmen were recruited, night control by means of patrolling trucks was introduced, and paid labourers were recruited from among the tail end farmers, to guard pipe outlets during the night.

This offensive met with strong resistance that was exacerbated by the fact that 1988–89 and 1989–90 were crisis years for the tail end section of the main canal generally. *Rabi*[29] 1989 was the first time that the cultivators in the distributary did not merely damage pipe outlets, but actually destroyed them. The fortified thread-gate is not easy to manipulate, so the farmers removed the gates and sometimes chipped away the concrete casing. In other cases farmers copied the keys of the gangmen and started operating the pipe outlets themselves. The gangmen, night labourers and night patrols of the Irrigation Department were bribed, outnumbered or beaten up by cultivators. In the absence of political and legislative support, the Irrigation Department was unable to impose the planned control. The tail end of the distributary moved further upstream.

In the tail end, the fortified thread-gates were damaged much less frequently (see Table 1): it makes no sense to manipulate the pipe outlet if there is no water. To go upstream and close all head end pipe outlets was an impossible and dangerous task for tail enders. With occasional strikes and the organization of 'functions' for politicians, the tail enders were able to effect short periods of water supply, but these did not bring them long-term victories. For most tail enders this was the signal to concentrate on other strategies to get water. Groundwater wells were dug in the red soils near the river. Lift irrigation with the help of motor pumps seemed to be the only solution for the tail enders.

Phase 4: *Rabi* 1990 to *Rabi* 1992
The Irrigation Department had overestimated its power but developments at the level of the main canal provided some relief. The water crisis of 1988–90 in the tail end section of the main canal led to changes in the management of the main system that increased supply to the tail end section of the main canal. Also, a system of rotation over distributaries was introduced, which increased the efficiency of water use. As a result, the average discharge into the distributary in the dry and hot *rabi* season increased and in 1992 was almost twice that in 1986. However, settlement and development of land for irrigation continued, and concentration of irrigation in the head region of the distributary intensified. By 1992 the tail end started at Km 21.

---

[29] *Rabi* is the second, dry, season; *kharif* the first, rainy season. The agricultural year runs from June to April.

The new strategy of the Irrigation Department seemed to be avoidance of conflicts with cultivators. The overall goal of pipe outlet operation shifted from implementing a reasonably *equitable* water distribution policy, to a *safe* water distribution policy with an eye to equitable water distribution, if equity could be achieved without risks. A new type of pipe outlet was designed that reflected the situation and the new strategy of the Irrigation Department: the ungated pipe outlet. It is an open pipe fixed in a head wall of granite stones. This pipe outlet does not have a gate, as this is considered as a waste of government money because the farmers will destroy it (see Photograph 8). The rationing/control aspect was realized in a different way. The offtake field channel was lined and constructed at a high level so as to lower the driving head of the outlet. In this way the Irrigation Department hoped to confront the farmers with a *fait accompli*. The only way to manipulate, besides rigorous destruction of the whole structure, is to construct checks in the distributary or sub-distributary, to raise the water level. At the time the field work was done for this paper, two ungated pipe outlets had been constructed. In 1992 the engineers were also considering reintroducing the pen-gate (without padlock), as this allows farmers to manipulate the outlets without damaging them.

Faced with damaged pipe outlets that could only be operated on an on/off basis, the Irrigation Department devised another water distribution policy.

Photograph 8 *The ungated outlet*

On each sub-distributary and the distributary itself, the head reaches are irrigated during the day time. At night every upstream pipe outlet is guarded by two labourers recruited from tail end villages. A truck and jeep perform night controls to check that all upstream pipe outlets are closed in order to push water to the tail at night. The Irrigation Department is concentrating its efforts on the pipe outlets taking water directly from the distributary, and on the sub-distributary intakes. The remaining outlets are left to their own devices.

This approach suffers from the same problems of bribes and intimidation as the earlier ones. In practice, this water distribution policy is totally *ad hoc*. When large groups of discontented farmers come to the office, extra controls are installed and the engineers try to show their commitment. When Irrigation Department officials are outnumbered by farmers at night at a particular point, they shut their eyes and turn their backs. When local members of parliament request them to supply water to a particular group of farmers, they try to do so for some time. Gangmen are bribed on a large scale or forced under physical threat to open gates and keep such things secret from checking officials. During night controls the Irrigation Department jeep first drives a 'warning' round before actually checking the situation. This is done to give the sleeping labourers guarding the outlets time to wake up and close the pipe outlet before the arrival of the checking officials. After the check the gates are re-opened. The actions of the Irrigation Department have become almost symbolic.

The description of these four phases shows that the pipe outlets and their technical characteristics are both an instrument in the struggle between Irrigation Department officials and farmers over water distribution and an outcome of that interaction. The designs of the pipe outlets have been modified in response to the balance of forces between officials and farmers. The different types of pipe outlets found in the distributary are indeed signposts of different phases of struggle. Pipe outlets are not only sites of social interaction, they also shape it and are shaped by it.

Conclusions and recommendations

These case studies show that the interface between farmers/water users and government officials regarding water distribution in large irrigation systems is both social and material. Pipe outlets as technical devices linking the distributary to the tertiary are socially constructed, and condition social interaction. The chapter shows that an approach to irrigation as a socio-technical phenomenon is appropriate not only for small, farmer-managed irrigation systems, but equally for large, jointly managed systems. The social and the technical dimensions of the system differ with each type of irrigation.

In the large canal systems of South India it is the state, through its Irrigation Department, that owns the irrigation infrastructure. It bears exclusive responsibility for its maintenance and for the delivery of water to farmers in the outlet *ayacuts*. Farmers have no formal responsibility for operation and maintenance, except within the outlet *ayacut*. Furthermore, in the Indian administrative system, there are no formal relations of accountability between water users and the irrigation bureaucracy. There are precisely defined legal mechanisms by which the government can correct deviations from the planned pattern of crops and water distribution, but the legal status of water rights for farmers implied in the 'localization' approach is unclear. Apart from this, the last example suggests that the effectiveness of such legal mechanisms depends on political support. Lastly, the command areas of the canal and the distributaries are so big that accountability between farmers living in different parts is absent.

Although the Irrigation Department is unable to implement the formal management structure and effectuate its formal authority, and although many farmers are unable to materialize their formal entitlement to water, the result is not anarchy. There is more structure and regularity to the process than in a Hobbesian struggle of all against all. To discover the rules governing water supply, the primary point of entry should not be property rights in water (and land and infrastructure), but more generally the social and technical relations that determine who exerts water control'.[30] The social relations have to do with relations between state and citizens and the ways in which politicians mediate between them and with relationships among agrarian producers regarding landholding, credit, employment and the like. The paper suggests that these relations are important and complex, although it touches on them only briefly.

In our view, these case studies suggest a need to develop a political economy of irrigation starting from the notion of 'water control'. Such an approach should relate three notions of 'control' to each other: the technical control of the engineer, the managerial control of the management scientist, and the political economist's notion of control as domination. The way in which property rights in water, land and infrastructure are articulated is one dimension of this more comprehensive notion of water control.

---

[30] We thank Paul Hoogendam for discussion on this issue.

3. Intervention in irrigation water division in Bali, Indonesia

A case of farmers' circumvention of modern technology[1]

LUCAS HORST

All Balinese rice-growing farmers are members of agro-socio-religious associations called Subaks. The Subak water division technology consisted on the one hand of institutional arrangements backed by temple priests and on the other of on-line weirs dividing flows into negotiated shares. In the 1980s, the Bali Irrigation Project (BIP) attempted to replace the weirs by adjustable structures to be set and reset on the basis of frequent calculations of the crops' water requirements.

The imposition of this technology was based on social and political preference, not on economic considerations. It produced conflicts between Subak farmers and the BIP. A situation was created that could not be handled by the irrigation agency. It was caused by a combination of circumstances: management transfer from the temples to the agency; the shortage of operation and maintenance staff; the highly variable field conditions; the lack of transparency and the complexity of the water division structures; and the method to calculate crop water requirements. The Subaks responded by: building Subak-type division weirs upstream of the BIP structures; breaking or removing the BIP structures; or approximating the original shares arrangement. Their responses lay bare the project's ignorance of local allocation and distribution principles. This chapter discusses water division structures as materializations of principles to allocate water. The adjustable structures introduced by outsiders are compared with the fixed structures developed by farmers. The chapter concludes with an argument about why Subak technology is not necessarily inferior to the project's technology, given Bali's hydrology, topography, soils and agriculture.

Background

Throughout the ages irrigation societies in Bali, called Subaks, developed a water division technology based on continuous flows and fixed proportional division of irrigation water. The watershares are in general determined by a combination of the sizes of the areas to be irrigated and mutual agreements.

---

[1] Technology is here defined in its broadest sense, pertaining to structures, activities related to construction, operation, reconstruction and related knowledge and skills.

This development, embedded in a cultural and religious environment, led to a sustainable irrigated agriculture, where farming systems were matched with hydrological and pest control boundary conditions. Priests and temples play a predominant role in the coordination and regulation of the water distribution within Subak societies as well as between Subaks sharing the same watershed.

This situation has been disrupted by two events. The first was the arrival of the Green Revolution in Bali in the 1970s where high-yielding rice varieties were forcefully introduced. This introduction resulted in pest explosions and increased use of pesticides, a change of planting and harvesting times mismatching the original religiously and ecologically determined dates, and finally a farming system incompatible with the centuries old agricultural practices. (For a vivid and well documented account of these developments the reader is referred to Lansing, 1991.)

The second event happened towards the end of the 1970s when plans emerged to modernize the Subak systems. The Asian Development Bank (ADB) and foreign consultants became involved and the Bali Irrigation Project (BIP) was started. This intervention by the BIP had two important consequences on Subak irrigation. In the first place, the Project ignored the coordinating role of the Subak temples and priests in terms of water allocation and distribution; the power of the priests, already weakened by the Green Revolution was further eroded by the BIP. The BIP was not able to create an adequate alternative (government) organization for the allocation and distribution of water.

Secondly, with regard to water division, a blueprint technology was introduced based on crop water requirements and hydraulic efficiencies as practised on Java. Gates were installed to regulate and measure flows instead of the Subak principle of fixed proportional division of flows. In general this technology has not been accepted by the Subaks. They handled the gates to accommodate the division of water according to their perceptions of water allocation, broke the gates, removed them or reconstructed the structures to restore the former fixed proportional division. Towards the end of the BIP the engineers gave in, reluctantly accepted the Subak water division technology and started to build fixed proportional division structures instead of gated structures.

Much has been written on the social, institutional and legal aspects of the Subaks (Geertz 1967 and Liefrinck 1969 before BIP, and Sutawan 1987, Lansing 1991 and Pitana 1993 after the BIP). The change of technology by BIP in terms of water division and the incompatibility of the BIP technology with the traditional Subak methods has been much less documented. This is remarkable since water division technology (allocation, distribution and structures) constitutes the core of irrigation: the water division structures are the tangible evidence of agreements (or disagreements) on the allocation principles. These principles are based on equity considerations,

Crops, people and irrigation

farmers' contribution, physical boundary conditions, agricultural practices, power structures and negotiations. One writer, Bellekens (1994: 157–9) reported on the modifications of BIP structures by farmers, though without giving a value judgement on the BIP technology. Also the process of technological change and the actors involved was not discussed. This paper intends to fill up the spaces which Bellekens left.

Methodology

This case study was carried out during three visits to Bali in the period 1992–4. Reports on design and operation of the BIP structures were studied and discussions held with engineers of the Directorate General of Water Resources Development (DGWRD) and staff members of the Udayana University of Denpasar.

Field visits were made to some twenty irrigation systems, most of them 'improved' by the BIP. During these visits the type and operation of the water division structures were observed and operators and Subak members were interviewed.[2]

Secondary information was gathered in the form of research reports and papers related to Bali irrigation.

The Subak organization

There are about 1300 Subaks in Bali covering approximately[3] 110 000 ha. The areas of the various Subaks range from a few hectares to over 700 hectares (Bali Public Works Office 1972).

The Hindu-Balinese religion and the tradition of communalism are the social basis of two distinct religious hierarchies: the Banjar and the Subak (Lansing 1991). The Banjar stems from the former kingships and is village-based while the Subak is an association of rice-growing farmers and is determined by irrigated land and water.

Lansing (1991) describes the network of water temples that spans entire watersheds where priests play a crucial role. He points out that two requirements for rice irrigation work against each other: optimal water allocation requires staggered distribution timing, but pest control requires

[2] I would like to thank Ir. Soenarno, Director of Irrigation I and Ir. Napitupulu, Chief of Subdirectorate Planning and Design, DGWRD Jakarta, for their consent with this study and the support given. I am also indebted to the DGWRD staff in Denpasar and district offices who gave me their assistance and time to make this study possible; to Ir. Jelantik Sushila former head of Public Works in Bali, I. Gde Pitana, Dr Nyoman Sutawan and Mr N. Sirtha for their information and support, Dr Steve Lansing of Princeton University USA for the stimulating discussions on the Bali Subak, and Subak leaders and farmers interviewed.
[3] The number of Subaks and the areas covered in the various references differ, but remain in the same order of magnitude.

that all fields in a large area be planted and harvested at the same time. The balancing of the two requirements to achieve optimal scheduling determines the agricultural calendar in the area. Decisions on crop calendars and water distribution are taken in the water temples on which the Subaks depend and they assume a ritual form that emphasizes the hierarchical interdependence of all levels in a watershed (Lansing 1991).

In spite of the complex topography, hydrology and soil characteristics on the island, this socio-religious Subak institution was able to develop, through the centuries, irrigated rice terraces into a sustainable agriculture. (For more detailed information on the Subak institutions the reader is referred to Sutawan 1987, Pitana 1993 and Lansing 1991.)

The Subak technology

Components of the physical infrastructure
Generally, the physical infrastructure of a Subak (see Figure 1) is composed of:

- a weir in the river
- a tunnel (or in less steep terrains, a contour canal) leading to the irrigable areas

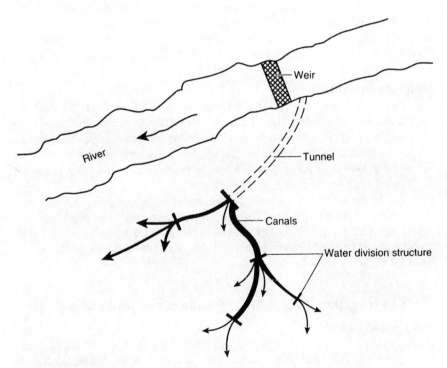

Figure 1 *Subak infrastructure*

- canals of diminishing size
- water division devices

The lay out, dimensions and sizes of the Subaks depend primarily on the topography, soil types and hydrology. It should be noted that the topography of the island generally precludes the building of storage dams. Furthermore, there is a difference in hydrology between South and North Bali: whereas in the South most rivers are perennial, the North has less rainfall and a more pronounced dry season causes most rivers to run dry.

Water allocation and distribution

Water allocation and distribution *among* subaks is generally based on the size of the Subak (Sutawan 1987). *Within* a Subak, allocation and distribution are related to the water share entitled to each member of the Subak. This share is called 'tektek' meaning 'cut into pieces'. It is primarily determined by the area to be irrigated and the member's contribution to the development of the Subak. Also other factors might be included in the sharing of water such as soil quality (percolation) and distance of the plot from the source (seepage losses in the canals). See also Pitana, 1993.

The principle of water allocation and distribution is based on continuous flows, fixed proportional division and mutual agreement between users and groups of users, although sometimes other arrangements are made and also certain forms of rotation (during dry season) might be encountered.

Water division structures

The water is divided proportionally by building overflow weirs for each of the bifurcating flows (see Figure 2). The weirs are placed in line perpendicular to the canal flow direction. Each weir has the same crest elevation d, while the widths a and b are based on the predetermined ratios of the bifurcating flows. These ratios a:b might be based on irrigable areas or negotiated between parties (see above).

It should be noted that turbulences are reduced by widening the oncoming canal, while by placing the overflow weirs on line, the velocity directions remain parallel. Originally these structures were all built in wood and/or bamboo (see Photograph 1). Nowadays mostly concrete is used (see Photograph 2).

The Bali Irrigation Project (BIP): the plans and justification

The pre-BIP period

Already during colonial times technical interventions in the Subak systems took place. From 1925 the Dutch tried to improve the physical Subak systems by building permanent weirs in the river and rehabilitating main

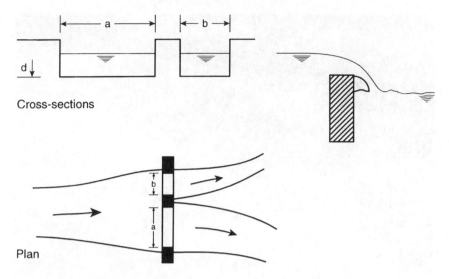

Cross-sections

Plan

Figure 2   *Proportional division of water*

Photograph 1   *Structure in wood*

Photograph 2   *Structure in concrete*

canals. After independence this policy was continued and improvements reached 35 000 ha by 1969 (Sushila 1984). It should be noted that these interventions did not concern the water division infrastructure of the Subaks.

Whereas those interventions took place piecemeal, the government felt that the introduction of the Green Revolution during the 1970s made the time ripe to improve Subak systems on a project scale. The Bali Irrigation Project (BIP) was conceived and the Asian Development Bank approached for financing.

Assessing the various plans

Before embarking on the first phase of the BIP, a team of ADB and Indonesian experts carried out a study to assess the scope of the project (Bali Irrigation Study Team 1977). Although no economic justification was found, the project was considered justified in terms of social and political preferences (ibid.: C-99).

On the basis of this Irrigation Study two foreign consultants, ELC-Electroconsult, Italy and ADC-Agricultural Development Corporation, Korea, drew up a Feasibility Report (ELC/ADC 1981) for the improvement of 130 Subaks throughout Bali (10 per cent of the total Bali Subaks). These Subaks were grouped into 35 schemes covering 17 500 ha. The improvements concerned not only the rehabilitation and extension of weirs and canals but also the rehabilitation of the water division structures within the Subak.[4] The consultants also studied the economic feasibility of the improvements and arrived at an overall economic internal rate of return (IRR) of 21.8 per cent. The impacts of the main improvements were described as:

- river water sharing and Subak coordination
- new rules for operation and maintenance (O&M)
- programmed cropping patterns
- use of measurement systems
- changes in cropping techniques
- yield monitoring systems
- taxes and water charges (ibid.: 3-22)

The BIP covered the period 1978–1986 and was followed by an overlap with a second phase; the Bali Irrigation Sector Project (BISP) from 1982 to 1989. This second phase contained the rehabilitation/expansion of 50 irrigation schemes comprising 19 000 ha. The type of intervention remained the same. Due to devaluation of the Rupiah, a considerably larger area could be covered by the Project: 76 Subak schemes, covering 29 000 ha (see Staff Bali Irrigation Sector Project 1990).

The Bali Irrigation Project: the proposed technology

The interventions of the physical irrigation systems by the BIP comprised:

- building of permanent weirs in the rivers
- improvements of tunnels and canal sections
- construction of water division structures to enable regulation and measurement of water.

These interventions constituted a large change in terms of river water sharing, water allocation and water division structures.

Building of permanent weirs

Many small Subaks had their own temporary weirs. These weirs, constructed with boulders and bamboo gabions, were easily destroyed by floods causing water shortages in the critical season and they required considerable labour input for rebuilding.

For economic reasons, the project replaced a number of temporary weirs by a single permanent weir. This required grouping of the Subaks concerned into one larger unit (Subak-gede or inter-Subak coordinating body).

---

[4] Other components of the Project such as water supply, roads and the Palasari Dam are not dealt with in this chapter.

Water allocation and distribution
Whereas the water allocation and distribution in Subaks were based on
principles of fixed proportional water sharing, the BIP introduced an
approach related to crop water requirements and hydraulic efficiencies.
In the operation and maintenance manual (ELC/ADC 1984b) the basis of
operation is 'the right amount of water for the crops at the right time'.
Cultivation of rice is assumed for the wet season, while for the dry season a
cropping plan is prepared based on a forecast of the water availability in
the river. For computation of the irrigation water requirements at different
growth stages of the crops and water allocation to the cultivated land, the
so-called 'Palawija Relative Factor' has to be calculated every 10 days and
the gates must be reset accordingly.

Water division structures
Contrary to the Subak structures for fixed proportional division of water,
BIP introduced movable structures to regulate and measure flows to
accommodate the Palawija Relative Factor irrigation scheduling. For
the first phase of the project a combination was chosen of a Romijn
weir as off-take structure and a sliding gate as cross-regulator (see
Photograph 3).
    This combination, often used on Java, appears to be the worst solution

Photograph 3   *Water division – BIP first phase*

Photograph 4   *Water division – BIP second phase*

for division of water, especially in systems where fluctuation of flows occur, as in Bali. The Romijn weir needs trained personnel to operate it. Soon it became clear that these personnel requirements could not be met. Therefore, different structures were adopted[5] for the second phase: sliding gates were installed to regulate the water and broad crested weirs were used to measure the flows (see Photograph 4).

Remarkably, neither the choice of structures, nor the change from one type to another have been discussed in any of the design reports or completion reports. Clearly, the project started with gratuitously copying the technology practised on Java and changed the technology without finding out the opinions and perceptions of the Subaks.

Bali Irrigation Project: impact

Ignoring the temples
It remains unclear whether the decline of the powers of Subak temples and priests is the result of a deliberate government policy or ignorance on the part

---

[5] The shortage of staff was given as the reason for change by the Bali officials of the DGWRD. Interviewed farmers commented on the incomprehensibility of the structures, while one irrigation official noticed the unacceptability of the Romijn weir for the ceremonial handling by priests: the priests have to 'open' the water which might be possible with a sliding gate but proved unsatisfactory with a Romijn gate being of the overflow weir type.

of planners and designers (or both). The weakening of the position of the Subak priests started in 1955 with the appointment of government officials to coordinate the Subaks and to collect land tax (Sushila 1984). This was followed in the early 1970s, when, with the introduction of the Green Revolution, new agricultural policies encouraged continuing cropping of rice and a shift to bureaucratic management of irrigation and cropping patterns. Finally the temples completely lost their control over cropping patterns and water allocation over most of Bali as a result of the BIP.

The report of the Bali Irrigation Study Team (1977) states: 'There is the need for improvement in the coordinated management of the water supply' and '. . . allocation among Subaks has to be controlled by some organization at a level above the Subaks, such as a commission or association of the concerned Subaks, or by the government'. Clearly the role of Subak temples was ignored.

At the start of the BIP, the Consultants dismissed this issue by stating (Feasibility Study ELC/ADC, 1981: 3-20): 'During recent decades the hegemony in Bali – Hinduism has gradually shifted away from the priest (pedanda) of esoteric tendency towards a modernizing intellectual tendency. The consequence of this change is a wider receptivity to the modernizing process, without provoking a rupture in religious beliefs and practices'.

However, by the mid-1980s a team from Bali's Udayana University, commissioned by the Department of Public Works, investigated and reported that 'the farmers were pushed to plant rice at the highest possible frequency each year, which gave rise to disorganization in water use'. The report emphasized 'the connections between the hierarchy of subak temples and cropping patterns' (Lansing 1991: 116). In spite of this mounting pressure on local officials to return control of irrigation systems to water temples, ADB and the consultants continued their path unaffected. Lansing found ADB and project officials to be of the opinion that water temples might continue to exist as religious institutions but their practical role in water management would inevitably disappear: '. . . to foreign consultants at the BIP, the proposal to return control of irrigation to water temples was interpreted as religious conservatism and resistance to change' (Lansing 1991: 115, 116). Significantly neither the consultants' reports on design and operation and maintenance, nor the ADB completion reports on the 1st and 2nd phase of the project contained any reference to this issue. Only at a late stage the Project Performance Audit Report (ADB 1988) recognized the role of the priests and water temples, and it recommended consulting them and seeking advice from them (ADB 1988: 49). The recommendations of the report however were ignored by the project officials of the ADB and the BIP.

Water allocation and distribution

BIP introduced a water allocation and distribution method based on the 'Palawija Relative Factor' (PRF). This method, stemming from the old

Pasten method developed in Java before the Second World War, was based on discipline and well-organized sugar operations. Although BIP claimed that this method is 'popularly practised in the Java area' (ELC/ADC 1984b), it proves to be an extremely cumbersome method requiring collection of a large amount of data by large numbers of administrative personnel and appears rarely to be working in Java (World Bank 1990, Horst 1995).

Not surprisingly, this method did not work on Bali either. A completely unmanageable situation was created by the combination of management transfer from the temples to the irrigation agency, the shortage of operation and maintenance staff, the highly variable field conditions and the lack of transparency and the complexity of the PRF method and the water division structures. As a result the Subaks generally took over the operation of the water distribution. The way in which the Subaks divided the water according to their needs in spite of the chaos created by the BIP is described below.

Water division structures – use and reconstruction
The water division structures constructed by BIP were designed to match the requirements of the proposed water allocation method (PRF) in that they were structures to regulate and measure water. The dimensions of these structures in terms of widths and depths of openings differed from the Subak structures. Whereas the original Subak structures had overflows with the same crest heights and with widths proportional to mutually agreed values, the BIP-structures had different crest levels, while the widths were based on hydraulic properties.

With the falling apart of the BIP water allocation method, a situation arose where the Subaks were compelled to revert to their former principles of water allocation (proportional division). By doing so however, they were confronted with the BIP water division structures which were incompatible with their own allocation principles. How Subaks solved this problem varied from case to case:

- In some schemes the gates were used on the basis of experience gained, approximating as closely as possible the proportional division principles (for instance, the Ababi, Sampalan left bank and Empas schemes);
- In other cases the gates were broken or removed and sometimes the openings readjusted (such as the Chengcengan scheme);
- Finally, in a number of schemes, Subaks managed to come to an agreement with the irrigation officials to rebuild the structures at the Subaks' costs. By building a proportional weir upstream of the bifurcation point the formerly agreed division was re-established (this occurred with Joanyar, Tiyingtali, Penarukan and Sampalan right bank schemes). Examples are indicated in Photographs 5 and 6. Photograph 5 gives a clear example of the difference between BIP-design and Subak perceptions in terms of width proportions of the structures.

Photograph 5   *Reconstruction*

Coming full circle

After 1986, towards the end of the second phase of the BIP, the project staff conceded that the water division technology of regulation and measurement of flows determined by the 'Palawija Relative Factor' method had failed. Shortage of staff and incompatibility between design assumptions and farmers' perceptions resulted in the operation of the structures in a way which was different from the project intentions. The project complied with the wishes of the Subaks and started to build the water division structures as fixed proportional flow dividers (such as the Ringdikit and Kapal schemes). See Photographs 7 and 8.

Photograph 6   *Reconstruction*

Photograph 7   *BIP last phase: proportional division*

Photograph 8   *BIP last phase: proportional division*

In the eyes of the BIP officials, however, this return to the original Subak water division technology should not be considered as the final solution for irrigation in Bali. The present technology based on proportional division is regarded as the last intermediate stage towards irrigation based on crop water requirements and regulating and measuring structures: it is only a question of time to train operational staff and farmers. The wisdom to pursue this technology is discussed later in this chapter.

The Bali Irrigation Project in retrospect – the actors

Although the economic targets as expected in the feasibility studies were not attained, the BIP did have a positive outcome: agricultural production increased while the required labour for weir maintenance decreased. This positive result should however be considered to have been achieved in spite of the project rather than due to it. Clearly the BIP gave the finishing blow to sustainable Subak irrigation in terms of further dissolution of the management structures of the temples and disruption of the water allocation and distribution principles.

In order to understand better the changes in irrigation technology effectuated by the BIP, one might ask which actors played a role in and around the BIP, what their reasoning was and which internal or external factors influenced the design process.

Subaks

The technology introduced by the BIP appeared to be incompatible with the Subak irrigation principles both in terms of water allocation and distribution as well as the water division structures. Although the issues of informing the farmers and farmers' participation are repeatedly stated in a positive way in the BIP reports, in reality construction often took place without farmers' involvement.[6]

DGWRD – Bali Provincial Office

Although several local engineers doubted the wisdom of the BIP technology, the Bali office was not able to exert much pressure on the outcome of the project. The Java technology was adopted and the consultants had the backing of ADB and DGWRD – Jakarta.

Udayana University

The study carried out by the University in the mid-1980s on water temples and irrigation was mainly focused on religious, organizational and agricultural aspects and less on the water division technology proposed by the consultants. Critical voices from the University on the blueprint approach of the BIP however, led to a certain animosity between DGWRD and the University, but without effect on the Project.

DGWRD – Jakarta

The water division technology proposed by the consultants contained the usual approach for irrigation projects on Java. (Water allocation and distribution according to the adjusted Pasten method and water division by Romijn weirs and sliding gates.) The proposals therefore did not give any reasons for doubts.

ADB

From the various design, operation and maintenance and completion reports it becomes clear that the ADB project officers generally complied with the BIP approach. Different views on the project principles however, were expressed by the ADB Post-Evaluation Office (ADB 1988). The discrepancy is noted between the Subak principle of water sharing and the crop based allocation concept of the BIP resulting in bypassing or remodelling the structures. No consequences are drawn however, in terms of readjusting the water division structures to better match the water allocation and distribution principles of the Subaks.

---

[6] See ADB 1988: 12: 'The process of designing and implementing tertiary systems was also often done without informing the farmers, and this often resulted in inadequate structures and rejection by the farmers'.

Consultants

The Italian and Korean consultants had no or little knowledge of the specific Bali–Subak irrigation. This becomes clear from the feasibility study (ELC/ADC 1981): 'For optimum water use, *arbitrary allocation* should be eliminated and replaced by a rational measurement system of rainfall, river discharge, canal capacity, losses and irrigation requirements' (ibid.: 3-23, emphasis added). To describe the carefully thought-out, environmentally balanced, water allocations by the Subaks as 'arbitrary allocation' proves the consultants' ignorance. Another example: 'The present BIP improvement will introduce many new factors, some of them external, into normal Subak life, mainly in: water allocation criteria; crop pattern planning; cropping and irrigation techniques; measurement systems; and yield monitoring. In principle these new factors *are not in conflict with Subak tradition*' (ibid:. 3-24, emphasis added). Apart from the fact that the BIP technology affects the core of the Subak irrigation principles, the proposed technology, containing measurements and collection of data from an extremely varied environment, should be considered unrealistic; this is discussed in the next section. The position of the consultants, backed by ADB project officers and sanctioned by DGWRD – Jakarta appeared strong: no discussions on the choice of technology were deemed to be necessary in any of the design and completion reports.

Appropriateness of the BIP water division technology

BIP and ADB officials claim that the BIP irrigation technology will prove itself superior to the Subak technology when given sufficient manpower and time for training of operators and farmers. In this section this claim will be discussed by comparing the BIP and Subak technologies with special reference to water division (allocation and distribution principles).

Before comparing these two technologies one has to bear in mind that most irrigated areas on the island have to be fed by run-of-the-river (r.o.r.) flows. The topography of Bali, containing deeply cut rivers with steep slopes, generally precludes the building of reservoirs. Consequently, the irrigation supply is determined by the variable river flows. High performance will be attained when the demand curve (irrigation requirements) matches the supply curve (river flows).

Subak method

The Subak water division method is based on proportionally dividing the incoming flow from the weir site into the canal system. Fluctuations of incoming flows are automatically propagated to lower levels in the system up to the plots. In other words *all* the water below a certain maximum (Full Supply) is entering the system. Excess water is drained, while all remaining water is used. The proportions of water division are fixed and no data collection or measurements are required.

The areas to be irrigated and the types and planting dates of crops are determined on the basis of experience in assessing river flows and rainfall to be expected, soil percolation and crop water requirements. The optimal match between demand (irrigation requirements) and supply (expected river flow) is attained by staggered planting dates, crop rotation and rotational irrigation.

BIP method

Here the supply curve is the same as with the Subak method: the variable river flow.

The demand curve is calculated using scientific methods and techniques: evapotranspiration computed from meteorological data, statistical analyses of river flows and rainfall, percolation data etc. These data should ideally be determined for each plot and compiled in a composite form: the irrigation schedule. This irrigation schedule should be reassessed with the Palawija Relative Factor (PRF) and if necessary the water division structures should be reset every 10 days (ELC/ADC 1984b).

Here we arrive at the first problem of the BIP method: in view of the large number of small plots and the large variety of soils (percolation), crop stands and cultivation practices, an enormous amount of data collection, processing and dissemination is required to compile the irrigation schedule. Supposing, however, that in the future a sufficient number of trained staff will be available to determine the irrigation schedule properly, the second problem will arise: the supply from the river is at any one moment either larger or smaller than the demand calculated in the irrigation schedule determined by the PRF method. Because of the very frequent river flow fluctuations in Bali, the irrigation schedule should be modified with the same frequency (every one or two days) in order to pursue matching of supply and demand. The BIP irrigation schedule determined every 10 days by the PRF method is seen to be a fiction. Furthermore, the gates of the water division structures have to be reset in the same rapid succession. This resetting is necessary since the water division structures of BIP generally consist of sliding gates as check structures and weir type structures as off-takes. In such a case, fluctuations in canal flows will be propagated disproportionally through the canal system. This implies the need for a practically continuous presence of operating personnel. The frequent resetting of gates also means that the water delivery to farmers will be erratic, enhancing uncertainty among farmers.

From the above discussion, it might be concluded that the BIP method of water allocation and distribution does not appear necessarily superior to the Subak method. Both methods are based on anticipation of the coming river flows, and are therefore dependent on the vagaries of nature. It remains to be seen whether the quality of scientifically determined data by the BIP method will prove to be superior to that of the experience and local knowledge of the Subaks gathered during many centuries.

Afterthought on turnover in Java

Nowadays, the Government of Indonesia seeks to develop a programme for management transfer from the irrigation agency to the farmers (turnover). The present water division technology in Java (allocation and distribution principles and related structures) finds its roots in the colonial irrigation before the Second World War. This technology was developed within the context of: strict centralized water management, little participation of farmers and vested sugar interests. Although this agricultural, social, economic and political environment changed drastically after independence, this technology changed little.[7] Not surprisingly this technology rarely performs satisfactorily in Java (World Bank 1990, Horst 1995). Its cumbersome procedures for computation of irrigation requirements, data collection and monitoring on the one hand and the complicated operation of the structures on the other, will preclude an easy turnover. The question arises therefore, whether some sort of Subak technology might not be more appropriate for turnover in Java.[8]

In the previous section we have seen that the Subak technology differed favourably when compared with the Java technology (specially in run-of-the-river schemes) in terms of making use of the available river flows, simplicity, transparency and staff requirements. The often heard objection that the Subak technology works satisfactorily 'because of the different religion' is questionable: Muslim groups in Bali also practice the Subak system. Another objection that is voiced often is the required strong communal organization. This is exactly what the turnover programme is striving for. Strong communal organizations require a technology that the communities understand and can handle. The Subak technology therefore, might render the creation of a water users' organization more viable.

From the foregoing it is concluded that a Subak type of technology might lead to a more successful turnover than the present technology as found in most irrigation systems in Java.

---

[7] One reason why this technology is being applied in Java until this day might be found in the dominant role which consultants and donors played in irrigation development during the second half of this century.

[8] This question is far from new. The colonial law of 24 July 1918 included a chapter on the creation of a water users' organization ('waterschappen') and led to a proposal by Happé to learn from the lessons of the Subak in order to effectuate this law. No action followed and only after the 1929 crises Happé came back on this subject and published a paper 'Waterbeheer en Waterschappen' (freely translated: 'Water management and Water Users Organization' – Happé 1935). His arguments in favour of the introduction of the Subak principles in the Java irrigation were based on recognition of local farmers' knowledge, the simplicity and transparency of the Subak technology (contrary to the complicated structures used in Java) and economics in terms of requirements of operational personnel. His paper triggered a lively discussion, and sometimes derogatory counter arguments, without convincing the irrigation engineering establishment.

4. The materialization of water rights

Hydraulic property in the extension and rehabilitation of two irrigation systems in Bolivia

GERBEN GERBRANDY and PAUL HOOGENDAM[1]

The sociological notion of hydraulic property as developed some years ago has proved helpful for explaining the mechanisms underlying the functioning of irrigation systems.[2] It originates from research in Asia. Few, if any, irrigation experiences from other continents have been described in the literature.[3] In this article we demonstrate that the concept is also crucial for understanding the rehabilitation and extension of two farmer-managed systems in Bolivia. The case material shows a diversity of hydraulic property rights connected to different water sources. These rights steer the irrigation activities within the systems.

This chapter focuses on the differences in perception of hydraulic property by groups of farmers and some engineers involved in the process of an intervention. The intervention team unintentionally confused property rights by proposing changes in the distribution process and by building new infrastructure. Farmers considered this restructuring illegal and demanded that access to the newly created waters be integrated into their hydraulic property structure in a well-defined manner. For this integration, property claims over water that was already available had to be carefully considered. An inventory of the existing rights laid the basis for an agreement to divide the extra water in a way deemed legitimate by all users. On the basis of this agreement we argue that intervention teams may implement changes more successfully if they and the prospective water users negotiate the outcome in terms of property.

In the next section we summarize some insights, drawing on literature about hydraulic property in Asian systems. In the third and fourth sections, the systems under study are presented and an account is given of the hydraulic property relations that govern its operation. In the fifth section

---

[1] Gerben Gerbrandy is senior adviser in irrigation research at San Simon University in Cochabamba, Bolivia; Paul Hoogendam is lecturer at the Department of Irrigation and Soil and Water Conservation of the Wageningen Agricultural University, the Netherlands (postal address: Nieuwe Kanaal 11, 6709 PA, Wageningen, the Netherlands).
[2] We refer to the sociological notion of hydraulic property. It should not be confused with the soil physics notion to indicate the hydraulic conductivity and water retention characteristics of soils.
[3] One exception is Diemer and Huibers (1992), who mention the concept of hydraulic property as a possibly valuable concept to explain features of the Senegalese systems they describe, but do not elaborate its content for that case.

we discuss the technical proposals for improvement and the sixth section describes the events that occurred during construction and indicate that the artifacts proposed would disrupt property rights and the operating systems based on it. The next section describes how farmers' protests and later extensive discussions have brought about the process of homogenization of water rights necessary for the future operation of the systems. In the last section we draw some conclusions regarding the need to integrate matters of property into the intervention in existing irrigation systems.

Hydraulic property under discussion

In the last 20 years much research has been devoted to the topic of property rights to natural resources. In the early 1980s this work came to include irrigation under the heading of hydraulic property (Coward, 1986a).[4] The concept refers to two sets of relations. First, the relations between people and irrigation facilities (water sources, infrastructure and the irrigation water itself) and second, the relations between the people who share access to these facilities or compete for their use.

In the literature, property rights are identified as the basis for water distribution, water use and the maintenance of irrigation systems. The discussion largely concerns farmer-managed irrigation systems: diverse patterns of hydraulic property have been encountered in these systems.

Several authors use the concept of hydraulic property to explain principles underlying the functioning of irrigation systems (Coward 1986a, 1986b, Hecht 1990, Abeyratne 1990, Pradhan 1987). They describe interesting processes that fall under the heading of hydraulic property without defining the concept clearly. The general reasoning is as follows; irrigation development comprises the construction of objects (dams, weirs, canals) through the investment of labour and/or capital by farmers, state agents or development institutions who thereby obtain a claim over the use of these objects and can exclude non-investors. Since certain individuals or groups claim property rights to these objects and to their use, these objects are called property objects.

The essential element of hydraulic property, however, is the relations among people that arise from these people's relations to these objects. The investment process entails not only creating people–object relations but also creating relations between the actors/investors. Hence, during the investment process, the relative positions of individuals with respect to the property objects and the use of these objects are defined, and thereby

---

[4] In the 1986 article reference is made to an earlier paper on hydraulic property (Coward, 1983, *Property in Action: Alternatives for Irrigation Investment*, paper presented at Workshop on Water Management and Policy, Khon Kaen, Thailand) to which we have not had access.

the positions of each investor relative to the others are defined. These relations are called property relations. They are found to constitute the social basis for collective action in various irrigation tasks (Coward 1986b).

Looking at irrigation development through the prism of property relations has led to two interesting observations. First, a direct link has been identified between the construction and operation of irrigation systems. During the construction process, property relations are created among the water users, and water rights are established. These relations are important for the execution of irrigation activities. Abeyratne (1990: 2) states that 'only if property rights in land, water and the irrigation works are clear-cut, will water users be able and willing to take full and effective responsibility for the operation and maintenance of the system'. In this definition, the maintenance of the system is highlighted. In terms of property, maintenance not only involves the maintenance of the physical infrastructure, but also the upkeep of property rights: in many systems, abstention from maintenance work results in the curtailment of one's access to water.

Second, the concept of hydraulic property points to aspects that are of special relevance to external (often public) investment in irrigation systems. Outsider investment in irrigation infrastructure is an act of property creation that interferes with prior property relations. Coward points out that:

> If state investment occurs in settings with existing community irrigation facilities . . ., the usual property consequence is the destruction of existing relationships. That is, property relations built around the prior investment process and the property objects that have been created are disputed, confused and muddled to the extent that they no longer serve to organize social action. (Coward 1986a: 499)

In descriptions of several intervention processes such, often unintentional, mixing up of property rights causes water users to oppose the intervention. It leads to problems during construction and to confusion and disputes after implementation (Hecht 1990: 62, Pradhan 1987). Project staff, whether dependent on the government or on a non-governmental organization, rarely relate this opposition and these problems to property issues. In many working situations, technicians attribute the farmers' objections to co-operating in the implementation phase to unwillingness, whereas the farmers may be protesting about the fact that they have not authorized the interference in their property structures.

Several points have not yet been clarified in the discussions on hydraulic property. The exact content of the property rights is generally not defined: do property rights refer to usufruct, ownership or access (to name but a few) and can they be sold, transferred, inherited or exchanged, and if so, under what conditions and with whose permission? The relationships between the creation of property rights and contributions in investment are rarely specified. It often seems implicitly assumed that property rights are proportional to investment. However, we know of cases in which the construction and upkeep of infrastructure is divided equally among the users but water is distributed inequitably. Apparently, other relations are also at stake. This relates to another point: in the analyses, hydraulic property is rarely connected to the wider economic and social issues (such as access to other resources and labour) and to the issue of power (for instance, the power of holders of rights to defend these rights against outside claims). These wider connections are needed to understand the precise processes of creation and distribution of water rights, and the struggles over hydraulic property and its redistribution.

This chapter is based on research during the extension and rehabilitation of infrastructure in two Bolivian irrigation systems and it contains similar shortcomings to those outlined above. The data were collected during the intervention in the farmers' systems. It was the struggle about technical improvements that revealed the underlying property structure to the external agents of change, including one author. Because of this, we do not discuss the links between the creation of hydraulic property and the wider social context and processes of agrarian change.[5]

The irrigation areas before intervention

The two interrelated irrigation areas central to this chapter are situated on the spurs of the Andes, in the valley of Cochabamba, 40 to 80 km from the regional capital of that name (Figure 1).[6] The two areas, Tiraque and Punata, and their water sources are shown in Figure 2. The Tiraque area consists of one major zone called *Abanico* (alluvial plain) of about 1200 ha of irrigable land at an altitude 3200 m above sea level and some scattered minor zones totalling an extra 400 ha of irrigable land at altitudes of up to 3800 m above sea level. The Tiraque area is divided into 31 *comunidades campesinas* (farmers' communities), 16 in the major zone (alluvial plain) and 15 in the minor areas. These *comunidades* are simultaneously official administrative units and geographical units of farmers' organizations.

The main constraints to agriculture are the irregularity of precipitation in the rainy season, the shortage of water at the beginning of the growing season and the frost hazard for late crops. Average annual precipitation is 400 to 500 mm, rising to 1000 mm in the mountain range. Eighty-five per cent falls in the summer months (December to March). Irrigation improves

---

[5] These questions form the basis for a current research project on the dynamics of hydraulic property in the Cochabamba region.

[6] The term 'irrigation area' is most appropriate, since waters from different sources are used in the same region, but form relatively independent organizational systems.

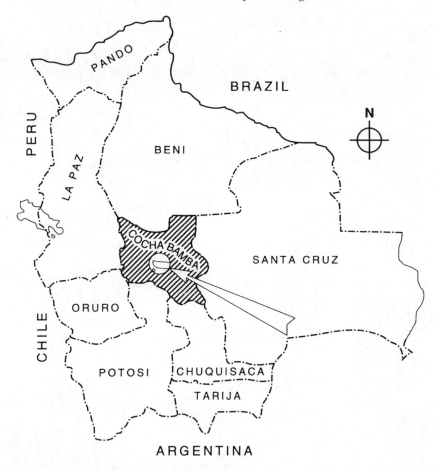

Figure 1 *Location of the irrigation area*

harvest security of rainfed crops by supplemental water application and enables a second crop to be grown. The main crops are potato, beans, maize and other cereals.

The *comunidades* have used the river for irrigation for a long time. They also exploit some natural springs. The discharges from these sources used to be at their lowest level early in the growing season, from August to December. During the 1960s, farmers from different *comunidades* dammed two natural lakes in the mountains – Lake Albert and Lake Clement[7] – to increase water availability. These reservoirs stored extra water for the

---

[7] The names of the reservoirs have been changed to ease understanding by readers not familiar with Spanish words. The Tiraque reservoirs are called Albert and Bernard, the common reservoir Clement and the Punata reservoirs Daisy and Eva (Figure 2).

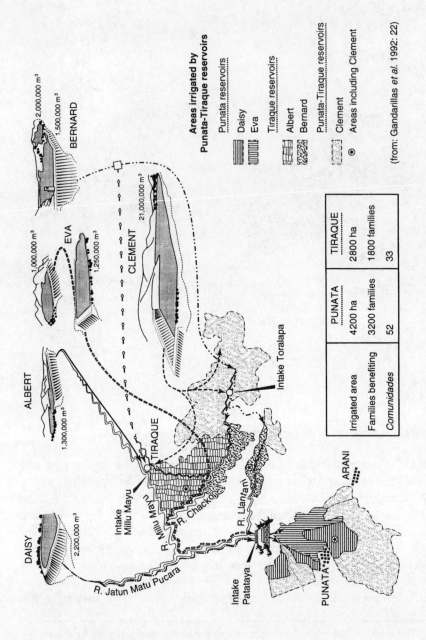

Figure 2 *The irrigation systems of Tiraque and Punata; areas and reservoirs*

(from: Gandarillas *et al.* 1992: 22)

	PUNATA	TIRAQUE
Irrigated area	4200 ha	2800 ha
Families benefiting	3200 families	1800 families
Comunidades	52	33

Areas irrigated by Punata-Tiraque reservoirs

Punata reservoirs
- Daisy
- Eva

Tiraque reservoirs
- Albert
- Bernard

Punata-Tiraque reservoirs
- Clement
- ⊛ Areas including Clement

following cropping seasons. Their water was directed to areas that were topographically separate and was managed in two independent irrigation systems: Lake Albert irrigated all 16 *comunidades* in the alluvial plain, Lake Clement irrigated 9 of the 15 southern *comunidades*. These *comunidades* thus had access to at least three types of water source: the reservoirs, the river and the springs. The remaining *comunidades* had access to only two types: the natural river flow and some springs.

With the construction of the reservoirs, two types of irrigation infrastructure could be distinguished. First, the reservoirs and canals to supply these with water, which were located in the mountainous zone, and belonged to certain groups of water-right holders. Water from these reservoirs was conveyed to the irrigated area via the rivers, together with the river flow. The second irrigation infrastructure is the distribution infrastructure in the irrigated plains. Water from all sources was distributed through a network of distribution canals, common to all water users in the area. There was barely any hierarchy in the distribution infrastructure; most canals served to transport the entire flow of up to 300 l/s and were also used to irrigate the fields directly.

Punata has a similar set-up. The Punata irrigation area lies downstream of Tiraque. It is also served by different water sources, and encloses an area of about 4000 ha, divided among 51 *comunidades*. In Punata, precipitation is slightly less than in Tiraque. Because of the lower altitude, about 2700 m above sea level, temperatures are higher and therefore water requirements are higher. Night frost occurs only in the winter months July and August. This makes Punata suited for nearly year-round cropping. The main constraint to intensive cultivation is the lack of water from June until November. The main crops in Punata are rainfed maize and alfalfa and irrigated vegetables and potatoes.

Like Tiraque, the Punata area used to be served by several sources of water: the river, the reservoirs and the springs.[8] During the rainy season all *comunidades* had access to the flow of the Pukara river, but in the dry season the number fell to about half, and these then shared the flow of the river on a time basis. Twenty-two *comunidades* constructed two reservoirs in the mountains and organized themselves into two reservoir committees to manage the use of these reservoirs. Each reservoir supplied water for its own group of *comunidades* without overlap. Lake Daisy, built in the first decade of this century, was the biggest, irrigating land in 10 *comunidades*. Lake Eva, built in the 1960s, was used in 12 *comunidades*. The remaining 29 *comunidades* had no reservoir water.

During the dry season the water from these reservoirs was conveyed to the head intake of the system via the river. In contrast to Tiraque, the areas

---

[8] In a small part of Punata tubewells have been constructed. They serve about 200 ha, spread out over the Punata area.

irrigated by reservoir water were not topographically separate. Water from all sources entered the zone through one head intake and used the same network of distribution canals to convey the waters to the groups of water-right holders. This implied that water from two or more sources might simultaneously flow through the river bed and canal sections and would subsequently have to be separated again in the irrigation area. To that effect the level of the original flow was indicated at a stone just below a division point before water was added from another source. When the new water arrived in the irrigation area, sufficient water would be diverted until the original level of the river flow was re-established.

Hydraulic property before the intervention

Many outsiders might expect that the simultaneous transport of water from different sources through a single infrastructure would create confusion and uncertainty about its distribution. In Tiraque and Punata, this was not the case. The waters from different sources were managed smoothly and independently of each other, even when they were transported through the same infrastructure. This can be understood only when it is realized that the distribution of water from every source was based on clearly defined property relations. Every source was linked to a group of water-right holders, who knew when and for how long a certain person had the right to irrigate. The group of water-right holders and the type of right they were entitled to differed per water source. Also, the investment they had had to make to obtain a right and the ways they had organized the operation of their system were diverse. To understand this diversity, let us take a closer look at the development and exploitation of the main water sources.

In the case of the river flow, the history of irrigation in Tiraque can be traced back to the Colonial period (mid 16th century).[9] Big land owners had their *colonos* (labourers) construct intakes and canals to divert water to their land holdings (Quiton 1985). The usufruct rights were assured through participation in construction and maintenance of the infrastructure by brigades of workmen from each *hacienda*.[10] The yearly labour input to maintain infrastructure and water rights was proportional to the water shares of the *haciendas*. The initial water allocation was probably proportional to the labour input in the construction of the irrigation facilities, since such proportionality is found in other irrigation systems in the Cochabamba valley. Shares were expressed in time: every participant

---

[9] This is particularly true for the river flow during the dry period of the year. After showers in the catchment area and during the rainy season, groups other than those indicated here also have rights to river water (see below).

[10] This contribution was called *mitha*.

was allowed to use the whole water flow for a certain number of hours or days. Rotations among the water-right holders usually lasted 21 days.[11]

In both Tiraque and Punata, rights to the base flow of the river remained in the hands of the land owners until 1952. 'Independent' *campesino* (smallholder) families outside the *haciendas* held no rights in these systems. After the 1952 land reform, large holdings were divided among the former labourers. Both the land and the water rights of the former land owners were assigned to the new smallholders. In many cases, land and water were divided equally among all ex-labourers of a land holding: each obtained an equal share of the total water share of the former *hacienda*. In cases where the land owners had assigned plots with water rights to their *colonos* through share-cropping contracts, the ex *colonos* consolidated these water rights after the land reform. As far as can be reconstructed, the water shares were not exchanged but merely subdivided.

Property rights to the reservoir water were also related to investment. The incentive to construct the main reservoirs was the increased demand for water. This increase resulted from an intensification of agricultural production that was itself the farmers' response to increasing land pressure and growing outlets for agricultural produce in Cochabamba. The increased demand for water did not lead to a redistribution of rights to the water of the sources but to the collective construction of reservoirs in the mountains. Farmers literally created new water and obtained property rights over it in return for their labour input. The future users agreed on how much labour each was to invest to obtain a share of the water, which was expressed as the amount of time that the full water flow could be used.

Expressing water rights in time shares had several advantages. First, the division in time proved a practical and transparent method to distribute water: no complicated measuring devices were needed and all other water users could easily check whether the proper person was irrigating and whether he was exceeding his period. Second, the division in time shares reduced problems related to the uncertainty about how much water would be available. Changes in water flow over the year would affect all water users proportionally, and thus good and bad luck were distributed equitably.

The exploitation of new water sources and the creation of new reservoirs provided opportunities for *comunidades* and their members to increase their access to water. Farmers could exploit different water sources and those with a great need for extra water were given the opportunity to contribute more labour than others, to obtain more water shares. This resulted in a variety of water rights among the farmers; some had rights

---

[11] Over time the word *mitha* also became used for the distribution system itself. Nowadays it is a well-known term designating almost all distribution systems for river water.

to the base flow of the river only, or to one of the reservoirs, others had rights to the three kinds of water sources.

The possession of two or more rights implied obligations to maintain the infrastructure used by two or more irrigation systems. In practice, however, the maintenance of the distribution infrastructure in the irrigation area was a communal task: the distribution canals belonged to everyone, and thus were to be maintained by all, even when some farmers used them more often than others. Since the groups of water users overlapped each other to a great extent, this practice never caused major frictions in maintenance.

The upkeep of the reservoir dams required more labour than that of the distribution canals. The maintenance of the dams and the reservoir supply canals in the hilly areas was far more demanding than cleaning the distribution canals in the relatively flat irrigation areas. This is one reason why farmers identify strongly with the reservoir systems. Their collective maintenance ensured the continued existence of the property object and re-established their interrelations.

Because the property rights are so clear-cut, there is no need for strong organizational set-ups. The formal organizations for the reservoirs mainly decide on the date to release water, and solve possible conflicts or uncertainties. The formal irrigation organization of the base flow of the river even went dormant for years. Only the water judges, who interfered in conflict situations, remained in recognizable positions.

The rules make water flows very mobile. The property rights of farmers are expressed in time and not related to fields. This allows farmers to move their water – during their turn – to nearly anywhere they want it. The well-acknowledged property rights also allow them to sell, buy and exchange water turns. Property rights as such may not be sold, although at present this sometimes happens.

Planning the intervention: the technical proposals

Although previously the farmers had extended and improved their irrigation infrastructure themselves, in the second half of the 1970s they felt a need for assistance. Outside help was required to increase the water supply by improving and constructing reservoirs in the mountains. Negotiations with the Bolivian government resulted in the formulation of rehabilitation projects that were part of the National Irrigation Programme and were financed by German Development Aid.

A feasibility study concluded that the irrigation facilities needed considerable improvements, although the farmers had merely requested more water. The project proposal consisted of an expansion of the water supply through the construction of reservoirs and of an improvement of the conveyance and distribution infrastructures. The idea was not to build a new system but to improve the existing one. Its layout had to be made more rational and hierarchical. For this, the usefulness of the canals to the improved system was evaluated.

The feasibility studies for the rehabilitation concentrated on hydrology, agriculture and agro-economics. No studies were done on water rights, and the organization to manage the base flow system was not identified. The water users' organizations were considered to be weak or absent, and their ability to guarantee an efficient use of the water was questioned. As a consequence, the idea of building upon the existing system did not include the social and organizational elements *in situ*.

A new organization was proposed, to be run jointly by farmers and government officials. It would also be an instrument to change the inequalities in water rights. The water distribution system was interpreted as unjust, since some farmers had rights to use water from more than one source whereas others had access to only one, or had no water rights at all.

The proposals were to be implemented via three projects. The first project concerned the Tiraque irrigation area, and consisted of:

- the construction of a reservoir (Lake Bernard)
- its conveyance infrastructure to the irrigation areas
- the improvement of the distribution infrastructure at the primary and secondary levels.

Lake Bernard's location made it possible to irrigate *comunidades* with rights in the command areas of Lake Albert and Lake Clement. This infrastructure was completed in 1982. The second project benefited Punata. It increased the capacities of Lake Daisy and Lake Eva, improved the distribution infrastructure and constructed one new main intake. The third and last project aimed at producing a major change in the irrigation systems. It intended to integrate all Punata and Tiraque systems by extending the capacity of Lake Clement from 0.8×10^6 m^3 to 21×10^6 m^3. Water shortages would no longer need to occur, as Lake Clement's capacity would be triple the capacity of all other lakes combined.[12] A new plan was to be established to improve the efficiency of the management of all water sources (rivers and reservoirs). Integration of all water sources into a single system would enable the water supply to be attuned to the water requirements of the crops proposed by market studies. It was assumed that farmers would agree to a delivery schedule and plan of operation based on the integration of the water sources, since water would be abundant after the projects had been completed.

To implement the operational plan it was suggested that water users' organizations be set up, for at least two reasons. First, farmers had to be

---

[12] The original proposal was to use the increased capacity of Lake Clement solely for Punata. Persistent resistence from Tiraque led to the proposal being modified to include Tiraque *comunidades* as well.

involved, to reduce operational costs. Second, farmers needed to be able to plan agricultural production correctly and to schedule water delivery according to the crop water needs. A technical assistance programme to train farmers and stimulate water users' groups was scheduled after the implementation of the new infrastructure.

Implementation: problems in construction and discussions over rights

To implement the three projects, a team of civil engineers, agronomists, economists and extension workers was assembled. Both project staff and future water users were to contribute in specific ways.[13] The project would provide technical assistance, construction materials and machinery. The *comunidades* were to contribute labour for transport and construction.

Initially, this co-operation functioned rather well. Later, problematic situations arose: on some occasions farmers refused to participate in construction works, objected to design decisions or obstructed the progress of the project. These protests seriously threatened the continuity of the project and forced project staff to discuss the problems with the farmers to ascertain the rationale of their objections.

The discussions between farmers and project personnel improved mutual understanding.[14] Farmers proved neither unwilling nor backward: they had well-reasoned objections to changes in their system. Their protests provide the key to understanding the functioning of the irrigation systems, the changes hidden in the technical proposals for rehabilitation and the reaction of participants. The events are especially instructive since their analysis provides insights in the creation and role of hydraulic property, the types of property relations and the importance of hydraulic property for collective action.

The smooth start
The project started with the rehabilitation and extension of three lakes, Bernard, Daisy and Eva. Work at these dams was arduous, because it is cold at the altitudes of these reservoirs, but the organization of the work did not create major problems. Farmers from different *comunidades* contributed to the construction, and representatives of the *comunidades* organized

---

[13] Throughout the chapter we present the project staff and the *comunidades* as homogeneous groups. In reality, there were differences within these groups. We acknowledge these differences, especially regarding issues of property, but consider that details would blur the line of the chapter.

[14] For an account of some important events and lessons learnt see: 'Dios da el agua; qué hacen los proyectos?', by Gandarillas *et al.* (1992). Especially Salazar in that volume for events related to labour participation.

their people and ensured that sufficient people participated. The *comunidad* leaders administered participation lists, as did the project employees. The only major complaint came from the project contractors: the efficiency of *comunidad* labour was low compared to paid labour. Two factors caused the delays and inefficient use of the time of contractors and hired machinery: the labourers were not always the most capable, and the work became an event that not only included working, but social and ritual activities as well.

The smooth start did not raise questions in the project team until later, when problems cropped up in labour organization. Then staff started to wonder why the start had been easy: the people causing problems had also been involved at that time. One main reason appeared to be that the improvement of the dams did not induce changes in the property rights. Without the project staff realizing it, only recognized users of the reservoir water had participated in these works; their work load had been divided according to prior standards and had taken place in the setting of their own organization. An important factor at the start was the farmers' faith in the project. The construction of the dam was a logical and clear investment in an obviously useful structure.

In terms of property, project staff did not realize that the construction work had the implicit effect of reconfirming individual property rights over these waters. In contrast to the reservoir users, the team members felt that the reservoir water had become a common good because the availability of water had been enlarged under the aegis of the project and with public money. The team members concluded that the water would fall within their remit for decision making and that they could direct it to farmers who had not participated in the construction work. This perception denied the property rights of the established holders of rights, and expressed the project staff's assumption that they, as representatives of the state/public good, were henceforth the new owners of the reservoir and were therefore entitled to decide on its use.

Conflicts about the construction of Lake Clement

The construction of Lake Clement was more contentious than that of the Bernard, Daisy and Eva reservoirs, for several reasons. The first was that Lake Clement was an extension of a shallow lake that was used by some *comunidades*. These were afraid they would lose control over its water and over the operation of the dam. The project's proposition to guarantee these *comunidades* an amount of water equal to the former reservoir capacity ended their opposition.

The second factor was that Lake Clement became an object of conflict between Tiraque and Punata. From the start, the inhabitants had had fierce discussions about how the extra water from Lake Clement should be divided. The project had proposed that all extra water be conveyed to

Punata. It excluded the area of Tiraque, because it had calculated that the area of Tiraque that would be irrigated with water from the reservoir was already watered sufficiently by the river, Lake Albert and the new Lake Bernard. In contrast, Punata still had a great need for extra water. If Punata could not count on Lake Clement's water, it would not have sufficient water available to irrigate the whole proposed area. This would threaten the feasibility of the entire project.

The people from the Tiraque *comunidades* opposed this proposal. Since Lake Clement was situated in the territory of Tiraque, the *comunidades* of Tiraque felt that they had priority rights to its water. Only water not used by these *comunidades* could flow to downstream *comunidades,* in this case the Punata area. Besides, the Tiraque people felt that Punata *comunidades* should not construct anything in their territory without their prior permission. In contrast, Punata *comunidades* demanded the full supply of Clement's water arguing that Tiraque had access to abundant water sources already.

The argument advanced by Tiraque reveals another aspect of property, namely that usufructuary rights to natural resources are normally based on socio-territorial control over catchment basins (see Plaza and Francke 1985, Sherbondy 1986). These socio-territorial claims were not shared by the project. In contrast, the project had created its own socio-territorial domain: the project area. All water in this domain was seen as a public good to be shared by all *comunidades* in the area delineated by the project. This project area cut through socio-territories and excluded Tiraque *comunidades* that would normally have priority rights over any new water that would become available in the Tiraque territory. The Punata *comunidades*, aware of the legitimate socio-territorial claim of Tiraque, made use of the project's conception to obtain access to additional water.

The implementation of the whole project would be at risk if Punata and Tiraque were unable to agree. After lengthy discussions, both water users' organizations signed a document drafted by the project. It specified the relative water rights of *comunidades* in Tiraque and Punata to Lake Clement's water, without detailing volumes. Immediately after signing, the Punata people openly tore up their copy to demonstrate its worthlessness to them. The *comunidades* had signed the document only to unfreeze funds for the construction of the new dam.

Reluctance to construct the secondary and tertiary canals
The construction of the secondary and tertiary canals was more difficult than the construction of the Bernard, Daisy and Eva reservoirs. From the outset it was difficult to organize teams of labourers, and when farmers saw the changes that project staff had 'staked out', their objections grew and their willingness to contribute to construction dwindled. Their main protest

concerned the layout and the dimensions of the canals. The layout was set up around hydraulic blocks of almost equal area and not around social groups. The canal dimensions were derived from the amount of water needed for the hydraulic block. The new canals had less capacity than the old ones.

Some problems and protests were linked directly to property, and others were linked indirectly. The former concerned the relation between labour invested and remuneration in rights to water. At the moment of construction no such relation had been clearly established, whereas normally the farmers would make *ex ante* decisions on future rights and structure collective action accordingly. The absence of clear agreements made farmers reluctant to invest their labour. Additionally, it was unclear whether the construction work on the distribution network would be included with the reservoir construction work, or whether the construction of certain sections would fall under the responsibility of a specific *comunidad* and not create water rights in the reservoirs.

The confusion about future property rights was aggravated by the uncertainty about the relation between new labour input and new hydraulic property on the one hand and earlier property rights on the other. Farmers resisted the project's idea of incorporating all flows into a single system. This was hydraulically feasible, but would, in Coward's words, confuse and muddle the property relationships. Even if agreement could be reached on the distribution of all flows, the variety of property rights over different water sources, and the related variety in labour obligations for maintaining the different systems made it complicated to determine how much labour different water users had to supply to maintain, secure or create their hydraulic property.

The farmers' protests that were linked indirectly to property rights concerned the layout and dimensions of the canals. Property rights formed the basis for the operation of the water distribution and were expressed as the amount of time a water-right holder might use the whole water flow.[15] The relation between property and distribution was clear. The responsibility for water distribution at the level of the *comunidad*, a recognized social organization, added to this transparency and to the means for control. A prerequisite for achieving this kind of distribution was that all canals had to be large enough to transport the whole flow of up to 300 l/s. Designing canals that crossed the territorial borders of social groups and had reduced capacities made it impossible for farmers to link distribution to rights.

Refusal to construct the intake and defence works of Punata
A different problem occurred with the construction works at and around the Punata intake. The project intended to replace the numerous intakes by a

---

[15] In general, water distribution is a good reflection of water rights. More detailed research is needed to identify deviations, their causes and their beneficiaries.

single head intake that would serve the entire Punata area. A new primary system would connect the new intake to the existing lateral canals. To protect the intake works from being washed out by huge peak flows, the river was to be canalized. This implied blocking off the ephemeral river channels crossing the irrigated area.

When they saw that a high wall was being constructed near the intake with the purpose of blocking the ephemeral channels of the Pukara river, inhabitants of some *comunidades* outside the project area objected fiercely. They argued that the ephemeral channels transported huge volumes of water during the rainy season and after rain. Their *comunidades* had a right to this extra water, using it to irrigate and to supplement groundwater. The farmers were afraid that they would no longer be able to exercise this right, since the capacity of the new inlet works and its branch canals would be insufficient to contain the entire discharge. Only after farmers threatened to dynamite the protecting wall did project staff capitulate and add gates to the wall to facilitate water inlets. These additions allowed the downstream *comunidades* to exercise their rights to this type of water, available at irregular intervals.

Claims from comunidades *outside the project area*

The final event that points to the importance of hydraulic property is that at a certain moment project staff discovered that 'unplanned' *comunidades* were starting to claim water rights. It became clear that contractors had not always verified the origin of participants and also that people from outside the proposed project area had contributed to the construction work and now claimed water rights. Their claims were supported by the water users' organizations for whom the consequence of the contribution of 'outsiders' had been clear from the outset. These extra claims put the project in the undesired situation of having to incorporate extra *comunidades* in the project.

The events point to the variety and complexity of property relations in the area. The project had not taken the property rights into account and unintentionally undermined the property structure by changing the property relations and by defining criteria for water rights other than the ones that the farmers applied. Besides, the project disturbed the transparent link between property and water distribution. The denial of rights and the loss of operating transparency incited farmers to obstruct the project's proposals that were based on the concept of one sort of water, to be used by any inhabitant. The farmers did not accept changes in their rights or in their way of operation without prior discussion. For them, discussion was crucial, as they assumed there were diverse rights and kinds of water.

Incorporating property rights in the intervention

The problems outlined in the preceding section have not yet caused a major change in the project's conception of irrigation water. The project staff realized that investment in construction and water rights were linked and that farmers reintroduced this link in the construction work. However, the project staff did not recognize that the water rights were former investments and they held to their contention that not only from a physical viewpoint but also from a management viewpoint all water sources should be collected into a single system.

After the first two phases, the project studied how the water from different sources was used, with the aim of modifying the plan of operation into one integrated system. These studies led to the feasibility of a single integrated water flow being questioned. Although the project had assumed that farmers would relinquish former reservoir and river rights and consider all water as part of an integrated and renewed system, it observed that farmers continued to use separate water sources and distribute water according to their former water rights. In the view of the project, this distribution practice obstructed efficient use of the irrigation infrastructure. Its staff contended that with a multiple source system farmers would never be able to supply the right amount of water at the right moment to all arable plots in the system. They maintained that it was essential for all water sources to be integrated into a single system. The project had elaborated a plan of operation that comprised a continuous supply from Lake Clement, which, together with the base flow of the river, would cover the regular irrigation flow. In periods of peak demand this flow would be supplemented with water from other reservoirs.

The question arose whether farmers would accept such an integration of old and new water. In the resulting discussions, property rights became explicit. Farmers insisted that former rights be acknowledged and the project staff had to recognize that they could not simply dismiss the water rights in the different water sources. It would also be difficult to integrate the former rights, because of the variety in sources, volumes of water per time share, levels of investment and exploitation costs.

In response to the problems of the unequal volume and value of property rights, project staff developed a process of homogenization. The intention of this process was that the shares from different sources could be compared and mutually exchanged. The first step was to express all water rights in volume instead of time, which was their regular expression. The second was to determine the price (in capital and labour invested) of a water share, per source. This was done using the lists of labour and capital contributed to each reservoir, which were always administered by the reservoir committees.[16] The price of the different water shares could be compared by expressing them as part of an equal volume of water. It became clear, for instance, that the water from Lake Albert was more costly than water from the other reservoirs. The price of the shares in the integrated system was based on the mean value of the shares of the former reservoirs.

After this homogenization process two issues remained to be settled: the number of shares each user could own and the number of days each individual water user had to work to obtain his new rights. The first issue was settled during a meeting of representatives of the water users from all *comunidades*. It was decided that only people aged 15 years and older could apply for water rights and that no water user could have more than two shares. The number of days a user had to work to obtain his new right was found by subtracting the labour and capital that he had already invested from the price of the new water shares. Since the volume of the new shares was larger than that of the former ones, the price of a new share exceeded even the price of the most expensive former share. Thus, everyone had to make a contribution to obtain a share, but the amount of the contribution differed according to prior property rights. Some water users had to work for only a few days to extend their prior rights, whereas those who had no rights in the pre-project situation had to contribute far more labour and capital. Farmers and project workers agreed that a portion had to be invested before the works were commissioned and that the remaining portion could be spread out over the next years.

As soon as the water users' organizations had agreed to the homogenization of water shares, the problems in the organization of labour participation vanished. The day following the agreement, several hundred water users came to the construction site. They wanted to fulfil the number of days required to obtain their right to a share of the water. Leaflets were distributed to enable every user to keep track of his investment debt. The administration via the *comunidades* continued in parallel.

In the perception of the project the process of homogenization was a success. It defined and clarified the linkage of water rights and investment. This was a crucial step towards the integration of all water sources that was judged necessary for the system to be operated on the basis of the estimated water requirements. In addition, one of the problems of water distribution was also solved. It was foreseen that it would be impossible to maintain the single flow operation. The flows in the integrated system (up to 800 l/s) would be too large to handle. The farmers' objections to the introduction of a division of the flow, that it had a negative influence on the transparency in

---

[16] The fact that reservoir committees had administered the contribution of all water-right holders shows their own need for a clear insight into investment levels.

operation, was overcome by the agreement to split the flow into equal parts. The clear division in time share could thus be maintained.[17]

However, project personnel overestimated the degree to which the homogenization had transformed the property structure. In fact, in the view of the water users, the former water rights persisted. Although project and farmers had agreed upon the calculation of new rights and on new investment inversely proportional to earlier investment, the farmers were reluctant to integrate all waters in a definitive manner. This reluctance became apparent when Lake Clement did not fill up to the level that the engineers had forecast. The volume of all water rights had to be reduced because of this lower level. The original shareholders reacted by reviving their former reservoir rights. Consequently, people without rights in the Albert, Bernard, Daisy and Eva reservoirs still could not obtain any water from them. At the same time, the small volume of water in Lake Clement was distributed in proportion to the recent investment in its construction.[18]

For some farmers the persistence of the former rights had been clear from the outset. They had always doubted that Lake Clement would be filled. The amount of water available differs over the years and hence so does the opportunity to meet the water rights. The weather in the catchment areas is too unpredictable to allow liberties to be taken with rights to different sources. Therefore, the homogenization should not be seen as a process of integration, but rather as a way to distribute access to new water rights. Most farmers have never considered it as a redistribution of former rights or as the basis for a renewed collective organization.

The reservoir committees of Punata and Tiraque that managed the reservoirs before the project still distribute the water today. They do so on the basis of property structures that evolved in the era before the intervention. The operation of the systems remains separate. Thus, the project was forced to do what it thought was impossible: it had to work out a plan of operation for the distribution of Lake Clement water that is independent from the exploitation of the other waters.

Conclusions

From the case material presented in this chapter we may draw the conclusion that issues of hydraulic property prove to be as important in Bolivia as in Asia. Property rights form the basis for the identification of water and for the operation of the irrigation systems, especially in the confusing situation

---

[17] Flows were not divided proportionally to the area of the *comunidades*, for this would have created different flows and reduced transparency. Instead, flows were kept the same, but the irrigation time per *comunidad* was varied, as it would be based on the number of water-right holders. When all the water-right holders of a smaller *comunidad* had completed their turn, their flow would 'help' irrigate the land of the larger *comunidad*.

[18] Because of the small number of days they invested, some farmers have a right to only a few minutes of Clement's water.

where various water sources are used simultaneously. Property rights define who holds the rights and who does not, and the relative access of each holder to the water from a particular source.

In line with the literature on this topic, we have shown that understanding hydraulic property is of specific relevance to intervention. It became clear that the issue of the right to water is related directly to investment in construction work. Indirectly, property relations underlie the operation of the systems and through this are related to the layout and dimensions of the distribution infrastructure as well. These inter-relations between property and infrastructure required a clear definition of future rights as a sound basis for investment and system management. This definition was arrived at through negotiations in and between Punata and Tiraque and between the project staff and water users. During these discussions and the later operation of the systems, it became clear that former rights persisted, largely because of the variation in the behaviour of sources over the years, and to the differences in the quality of their water. These differences stimulate farmers to gain access to several sources and avoid reliance on one only. Given this diversity, an insight into water rights and a discussion of these rights helped to define and regulate labour input and establish rights all users accepted.

The acknowledgement of an unequivocal relationship between labour input and water rights provides an important argument in favour of user co-operation in the construction of irrigation works. The case refutes the contention that participation is useful only as a means of creating a 'sense of ownership' in the users. Rather, it shows that labour input by farmers should be seen as a rational and deliberate investment that, like any other investment, requires future rights and gains to be clear. Understanding the relationship between input and rights also allows projects to initiate discussions on measures that make access to water more equitable.

5. Religion and local water rights versus land owners and state

Irrigation in Izúcar de Matamoros (west bank), Mexico[1]

MARC NEDERLOF and ERIC VAN WAYJEN[2]

Development of irrigation and intervention in existing irrigation systems have often been implemented as purely technical operations. Most irrigation projects have focused on the physical aspects of irrigated farming and have been oblivious to the social context of the technology that they have introduced. This attitude has had detrimental effects on the water users. Moreover, the agencies responsible for the irrigation projects often have not achieved their objectives.

More and more people are recognizing these problems and are attempting to address them. One solution proposed is that when an irrigation system is built, institutions should be set up simultaneously to ensure that it is run smoothly.[3] However, we feel that technicians often and all too easily ignore the local economic, social and cultural context of an irrigation intervention. Yet it is this context that determines how the water users adapt the intervention to their needs and views.

In this chapter we explore this idea with the help of a case study. We examine two communal irrigation systems in central Mexico that are over 500 years old and are situated on either side of a river near the town of Izúcar de Matamoros. Even though these systems have been associated

---

[1] This chapter is based on field and archive research done with T. Eilander in Izúcar de Matamoros, Puebla, Mexico, from September 1985 to January 1986, for our MSc degree in Tropical Land and Water Management at Wageningen Agricultural University. This research was inspired by the anthropologist J.A.J. Karremans from Leiden University, who had done research in Izúcar. In the archives of the *Secretaria de Agricultura y Recursos Hidraulicos* in the city of Puebla, we consulted: file 447.2/3 172-1: 1968-open: *Reglementacion de Corrientes, barrios Orientales*, file 447.2/3 172-2 part 1: 1968–1972, part 2: 1973-open: *Reglementacion de Corrientes, barrios Orientales*, file 447.2/3172-2 part 1: 1968–1972, part 2: 1972-open: *Reglementacion de Corrientes, barrios Occidentales*, file 447.2/3172 part 2: 1929: *Informe (sobre) reglementacion del Rio Nexapa*, by Ing. I. Santos Salcedo. This study about the irrigation along the Nexapa contains a transcription of a document from 1635, file 447.2/3 172 part 3: 1933–1934: letters about problems around the introduction of the *junta de aguas*. This same archive also contains the files of the Commission del Rio Balsas (1964–1966). Those consulted are: file II-3-5: *Reglementacion de Corrientes, Rio Nexapu. Municipios de Atlico y Matamoros*, file II-5-6: *Quejas y Conflictos de usuarios, Canal barrios Occidentales. Izúcar de Matamoros*, file II-5-7: *Quejas y conflicos de usuarios, Canal barrios Orientales. Izúcar de Matamoros.*

[2] At present, Nederlof is working in the Traditional Irrigation Improvement Programme in Tanzania and Van Wayjen is at the International Irrigation Management Institute.

[3] This is the organizational approach to irrigation which has been promoted by multilateral organizations.

with the Spanish government and with *haciendas* since colonial times, it was not until this century that technical changes were introduced by the Mexican government.[4]

From time immemorial, water rights have been separate from land ownership in the two irrigation systems. The system of the eastern wards (*barrios*) was reorganized by the government in 1966.[5] This involved making the right to irrigation water dependent on land ownership, as stipulated by Mexican law. In the irrigation system of the western wards, the farmers have successfully resisted this reorganization. Several features of the organization of the system on the west bank have, so far, been remarkably long-lasting. These include the linking of the right to water to the fulfilling of religious obligations, and an irrigation rotation that is independent of land ownership.

Below, after outlining the context of irrigation in the western and eastern wards, we will discuss the organization of irrigation in the western wards. It will become evident that irrigation is not only closely intertwined with other aspects of local society but is also at the heart of resistance to the capitalist mode of production. The latter instigates organizational patterns of irrigation that differ from those instigated by forms of farming that are less dominated by capital. The eastern wards are analysed by Timen Eilander in Chapter 6.

Location and physical environment

Izúcar de Matamoros has 50 000 inhabitants and is situated in the state of Puebla, 60 km from the city of that name and 150 km from Mexico City. It lies at an altitude of 1280 m in a valley that is wide and flat, surrounded by hills of up to 1800 m. Izúcar lies in the rain shadow of the highlands to the south and west, and this, together with its low altitude, ensures the area experiences a rather dry and warm climate where night frosts are very light. The rainy season lasts from mid-May to mid-October and mean annual rainfall is 900 mm. Annual potential evapotranspiration is 2200 mm.

Rainfed farming on valley fringes that cannot be irrigated allows only one harvest per year, and has scarcely been modernized. The crops are those of the pre-Columbian period: maize and beans. Some sorghum is grown to feed cattle; its cultivation is mechanized.

The hills surrounding Izúcar are steep and rocky limestone and are used solely for extensive livestock farming on a limited scale. The soils in the valley are on volcanic parent material. They are fertile and have a uniform slope of 1–2 per cent. About 40 irrigation systems tap their water from the

---

[4] A *hacienda* is a large farming company. It is usually owned by a non-Indian. The company labourers live on the farm.
[5] *Barrio* means ward or district.

Figure 1 *Location of Izúcar de Matamoros in Mexico*

River Nexapa which flows through the valley. Nexapa's water comes from the vicinity of a volcano 50 km north of Izúcar, where rain and snow fall abundantly. At the end of the last century a few sugar-cane *haciendas* along the lower reaches of the Nexapa had a tunnel dug through the hills at the upper course of the Nexapa to divert water from the Atoyac, a larger river, to the Nexapa. This tunnel increases the minimum flow of the Nexapa during the dry season from 4 to 7 m³/s.

History

Izúcar (a corruption from the Aztec name Itzocan) was a port of call for Aztec merchants en route to or from Tenochtitlan (Mexico City). Before the Spaniards arrived it already had a diversified, irrigated agriculture. Soon after its capture, in 1520, Dominican monks established a cloister to Christianize the region, but many pre-Columbian elements linger on beneath the Catholic surface.

The valley rapidly became known for its sugar-cane. In 1635 the colonial government divided the river water between nine diversion points. These were mainly the sugar-cane *haciendas*, but the Indians of Izúcar also were awarded the right to irrigation water. The *haciendas* could not take this right away nor buy it from them. In addition, the Indians were given the right to the land surrounding the town. This land did not fall into the hands

of the *haciendas*, not even in later centuries. The Indians chiefly lived off
the produce from the orchards and vegetable gardens (the *huertas*) and sold
only a fraction.

After the Mexican revolution (1911–20), the government began to
expropriate the *haciendas*, converting them into state-controlled co-opera-
tives, *ejidos*. Then the American consul Jenkins arrived in the valley. He
bought the *haciendas* that had become impoverished during the civil war
and established a sugar-cane empire of 50 000 ha and a large sugar factory
in Atencingo, 20 km southwest of Izúcar (Ronfeldt 1973). He also purchased part of the land belonging to Izúcar, notably the swampy areas,
which until the revolution had been communal property of the Indians who
used it as pasture. Jenkins succeeded because the population had been
reduced to poverty due to plundering during the revolution and had been
weakened by an influenza epidemic. And he was not averse to using threats
and force either. After the dispossessions, Jenkins drained large tracts of
land to cultivate lucrative cash crops.

Jenkins had considerable impact on agriculture in Izúcar. Through him,
inhabitants of the wards, often as farm labourers, came into contact with
new, market-oriented and large-scale forms of irrigated cultivation of new
crops and varieties. The subsistence agriculture of the inhabitants began to
use more external inputs. Gradually, their production became more market-
oriented.

In 1938, Jenkins' sugar-cane fields were expropriated by President
Cardenas and converted into one big *ejido*. The land was distributed
among Jenkins' farm and factory workers with the proviso that they
cultivate cane on all the land. The board of the *ejido* was appointed by
the government. Jenkins remained involved through the sugar factory in
Atencingo. After continuous power struggles the *ejido* was divided up in
1968. Today, these smaller *ejidos* still cultivate sugar-cane for Atencingo.

On Jenkins' death, in 1964, his land around Izúcar was divided among
his labourers and assistants. These lands have their own irrigation systems
and do not belong to the wards. In terms of the crops, types of ownership
and irrigation organization, the lands belonging to the wards form an island
in a sea of sugar-cane.

The centre and the wards

Izúcar de Matamoros is a regional capital and located at a crossroads with
the Pan-American highway. The present population is of mixed Indian-
Spanish origin and to a lesser extent of negro descent; it no longer speaks
an Indian language. By Mexican rural standards, Izúcar is prosperous but
there are marked differences, particularly between the centre and the
outlying wards (*barrios*). Many families in the wards have one or more
members working in Puebla, Mexico City or the United States. This is

obvious from the long queue by the dollar exchange counter at the post office.

Izúcar consists of a centre and 14 wards (*barrios*), divided into two groups of seven. The centre lies on the west bank of the Nexapa along with the seven western wards which lie close together to the south of the centre. On the east bank, the seven eastern wards stretch along the river. The Nexapa flows from north to south. In the centre, the most important economic activities are trade and services. The wards are more agricultural and more traditional. They are not as densely populated as the centre and include *huertas*, woodland-like areas with fruit trees, other trees, shrubs and vegetable gardens.

Until the beginning of this century, only people of Spanish descent and *mestizos* (people of mixed Spanish/Indian origin) lived in the centre, and the inhabitants of the wards were Indians. Nowadays people from the centre still tend to look down on the inhabitants of the *barrios* and sometimes refer to them by the derogatory name *barriecos*. The inhabitants of the wards differ from those in the centre not only because of their agricultural activities but also because of their income, their education, their clothing, and most of all their religious traditions.

The water-right holders in the wards have a distinct socio-economic image: they pride themselves on being self-supporting farmers, *campesinos*. They look down on the members of the surrounding *ejidos* as being no more than labourers (*peones*) and distinguish themselves from the big farmers whom they call *agricultores* or *capitalistas*.

The wards

The notion of 'ward' (*barrio*) usually refers to a group of houses that has some status in public administration. The inhabitants of Izúcar's *barrios*, for instance, choose an *inspector* from their midst to represent them on the municipal council. In the case of Izúcar, the wards on both banks also play important roles as organizational units in irrigation and as religious units: the inhabitants of a ward feel bound to a ceremonial centre. In this section we will pay some attention to these two non-administrative aspects of the wards.

Each ward has a church dedicated to the saint after whom church and *barrio* are named (see Figure 2). The inhabitants of a ward feel committed to their saint. They are bound to serve him or her, for example, by contributing to religious banquets, masses and processions and to the maintenance of the church. Most inhabitants of the ward, however, do not fulfil these obligations strictly. On the west bank, only a group of people in each ward takes this obligation seriously. This group is made up of people who have rights to irrigation water. They are referred to as *usuarios*, water-right holders (literally: users) or *sirvientes*, which means

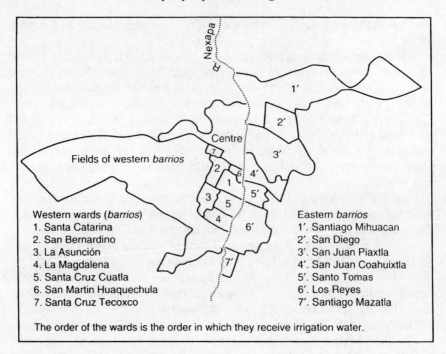

Figure 2 *Izúcar de Matamoros: the* barrios *with their irrigated fields*

servants (of the saint of the ward), or *los numeros*, because each ward has a fixed number of people entitled to water, either 16, 32 or 48.

The water-right holders explain that the right to irrigation water is combined with serving the *barrio* saint. They say that the water belongs to the saint who gives it to the ward and that in return they must serve these saints. A water-right holder does not necessarily live in the ward whose saint he serves.[6]

Every year, the water-right holders in a ward 'elect' a *mayordomo* from their midst. The honoured person is responsible for the church building, other property of the church and all religious activities such as the religious feasts – the biggest of which honours the *barrio* saint. Water-right holders and their families primarily take part in these festivities; the other inhabitants of the ward are less involved. The *mayordomo* finances these festivities, spending as much money on food, flowers and fireworks as he can afford. The water-right holders take fixed turns in being 'elected' as

---

[6] Formal religious organization as well as the organization of the irrigation are a man's job in Izúcar. Most holders of water rights are men. The few females who hold water rights have usually inherited these from their husbands and they allow a man (a son, for example) to work with the water.

mayordomo, although personal circumstances, such as a bad harvest, are taken into account. Recently, some wards have begun to share the expenses for the religious activities among the water-right holders. The reason for this is said to be rising costs.

In each ward one or two *principales,* elderly water-right holders who have fulfilled all official functions, have authority over the other water-right holders and the rest of the ward. They see to it that the traditions are upheld. Until the 1930s, the *mayordomos* and the *principales* together supervised the organization of irrigation. However, in 1934, within the framework of a new regulation for all groups of water users, the government introduced the irrigation management still present today: the *junta de aguas.* Since then the irrigation organization is formally detached from the religious organization but the *principales* still play their roles in the western wards, especially in the allocation of water rights.

In 1966, the government linked the right to water in the eastern wards with land ownership in these wards. Formal obligations towards fulfilling religious tasks were abolished, and the organization of the religious activities became less stringent. For instance, there are no longer any *principales* on the east bank. Other differences between the religious organization of the eastern wards and the western wards prior to 1966 are probable but have not been uncovered.

Even though there is no formal obligation, plenty of inhabitants in the eastern wards are still prepared to take the role of *mayordomo* upon themselves and to contribute to the expenses of the religious activities and the maintenance of the ward church. In particular, many (but not all) users of the irrigation water (also called *usuarios* in the eastern wards) feel that they have a moral obligation to do so.

Water-right holders are also obliged to serve in the *Cofradía del Santissimo Sacramento.* This is a brotherhood of 12 water-right holders who belong to one ward. Each year the *cofradía* comes from a different ward, alternating between an eastern and a western ward. There are five wards on either bank that each have a turn for the *cofradía,* in the same order as they receive irrigation water. The wards with the fewest water-right holders do not participate. The members of the *cofradía* collect money twice a week and use it to pay for a mass held once a month in the Santo Domingo, the principal church in the centre of Izúcar. The brotherhood is also responsible for the activities during Easter.

The *cofradía* symbolizes the unity of the 14 wards. The order in which the wards receive the irrigation water is the one employed by the *cofradía* and is reflected in other forms of religious observance. This is a sign that irrigation and religion have a common cultural background. In his structural analysis of the culture of Izúcar, Karremans (1983, 1987) shows that this cultural background contains pre-Columbian elements.

The two irrigation systems

The irrigation systems of both the western and the eastern wards each have an inlet in the river Nexapa. The systems irrigate the *huertas* and the fields around the wards. In the western wards the inlet is located to the north of the centre. The main canal runs partially through the centre and then branches off in the wards. The furthermost fields are 5 km from the first junction.

The inlet of the eastern wards is located 2 km upstream. They share their main canal with the Raboso *ejido*. At the point where the main canal enters the wards it bifurcates into a canal for the wards and a canal for Raboso. The Raboso canal first runs for 2 km between the fields of the wards and contains a few small aqueducts. The furthermost *barrio* fields lie 4.5 km from this junction.

Most canals are old and have no lining apart from the section in the centre. The main canals are about 3 m wide and 75 cm deep. Their average slope is 0.5 per cent and both canals are approximately 2 km long. The canals in the fields are 0.5 to 1 m wide and 25 to 50 cm deep. Their slope varies from 0.5 to 2 per cent, and therefore the rate of flow is greater than 0.5 m/s. This prevents silt being deposited and blocking the canals. The canals provide water for irrigation, as well as drainage for the surface run-off water.

According to rules set down in 1930, the western wards are entitled to 363 l/s. However, this flow varies between 1000 l/s during the rainy season to 220 l/s at the end of the dry season. The total area of the western wards is 700 ha. Since part of it has houses on it and another part is irrigated with pumped groundwater, about 450 ha are irrigated with river water. These figures show that water is scarce at the end of the dry season, a fact confirmed by statements from farmers.

The adduction canal of the eastern wards and Raboso is entitled to 950 l/s: 540 l/s for the wards and 410 l/s for Raboso. The apportionment is achieved by means of a concrete construction that divides the flow proportionally. The total area of the eastern wards is 550 ha. Here too, part of the area has houses on it, but no groundwater is pumped up. Therefore, just as on the west bank, the river water irrigates about 450 ha. The difference in flow is similar to that of the western wards (from 1300 l/s to 300 l/s). The eastern wards have a little more water that the western wards.

In 1985, at the end of the rainy season, the eastern wards temporarily reduced their share of the water by placing stakes in the division structure so as to avoid getting too much water. By contrast, the western wards used illegal means to get more water for their rice fields during precisely the same period. On the east bank, there are few concrete divison structures; in most cases the water is divided without structures, or with simple cemented division boxes.

Distribution of water on the west bank[7]

In the western system the water is distributed between the water-right holders in the seven wards. They alone have the right to use the river water that comes in. The number of water rights is fixed: 192 in total. The distribution of the rights among the seven wards is also fixed: three wards have 16 water rights, three others have 32 each, and one ward has 48. The possession of such a right is independent of land ownership. A person may therefore possess a right to water without owning land, a situation in which many water-right holders find themselves.

Each water-right holder may possess only one right to water. However, water-right holders frequently allow other such holders to act as their 'representatives', for example, during a long stay outside Izúcar. The 'representative' of the water right can use it as he uses his own. It entitles him to a second irrigation turn but also makes him responsible for the associated obligations. The water right remains in the name of the original water-right holder, who can claim it on his return.

A water right entitles its holder to a turn of six hours every so many days. During his turn the water-right holder has one *cuarteron*, which is one quarter of the main flow, at his disposal. He can do what he likes with the *water*: he can use it himself, lend it and even sell it. His water *right*, on the other hand, must remain intact: it may not be divided and on no account be sold. Consequently, a distinction can be made between the distribution of water rights and the distribution of water.

The body of water-right holders in a ward constitutes the most important organizational unit for the distribution of the water rights and also for the distribution of the water. At ward level the ultimate responsibility for all irrigation matters rests with the 'board of water-right holders' (*junta de usuarios*), the committee of holders of water rights in the ward. From their midst, in an order that is essentially fixed, two water-right holders are appointed for the day-to-day management of their ward for a period of three years. The 'ward representative' (*representante*) and his 'deputy' (*suplente*) supervise the daily routine in their ward, as far as irrigation is concerned. The ward representative has the more important position; the deputy carries out the tasks.

The ward representative represents his ward in the irrigation board of the seven wards. This 'water board' (*junta de aguas*) consists of the seven ward representatives. From its midst it chooses a chairman, a secretary and a treasurer to form a daily executive committee. The water board is responsible for all irrigation matters over and above the ward level, such as the

---

[7] The distribution of water in the dry season is organized differently from in the wet season, when wet rice is the main crop. For the purposes of this chapter we will ignore the wet period.

maintenance of the adduction canals. It also mediates in conflicts between wards. Furthermore, it represents the entire group of water-right holders to the outside world and especially to the government.

This set-up was introduced by the government in the 1930s as part of the new rules for distributing the water among and within the irrigation units along the Nexapa. The reorganization also meant the establishment of a link between the right to water and land ownership. Although the reorganization was accepted, the linking of the distribution of water to land ownership ran up against hefty resistance from water-right holders on both banks. They appealed to their age-old communal right and to the Revolution. They pointed out that injury to the smaller farmers for the benefit of the bigger land owners could not be reconciled with the Revolution. When the conflict reached its peak, the government service for irrigation was abolished because of political conflicts at the top. Even before this event, the government service for irrigation was weak. It did not have any detailed knowledge of the situation in the wards and had no money for the construction of a new, adjustable inlet. The service was also weakened by the fact that some employees found it undesirable to let down the small farmers.

Because the official set-up was taken over, the government considered the 'traditional' water distribution to be illegal. Nevertheless, it is this traditional distribution that the water board represents. This ambiguity has been normalized: each ward representative, even if he owns no land, receives formal credentials from the government in recognition of his position.

Distribution of the water rights

The authority to distribute the water rights of a ward lies within the ward in question. There are two ways in which an inhabitant can become a water-right holder: by inheritance, whereby in most cases the water right is passed down from father to son, or by being allocated a water right that has come free. In both cases, agreement must be reached between the water-right holders of a ward and the new water-right holder. The other water-right holders must be confident that the newcomer will do his best for the irrigation system and will fulfil his obligations. Often the heir has, for some time, been working with the irrigation rotation linked to the water right, allowing the other water-right holders to get to know him well.

The allocation of a free water right is a matter for decision by a special meeting of the board of water-right holders. Although a free water right is part of the total number of water rights of a ward, it does not stand under the name of an individual. A water right can become free if there is no heir, if a water-right holder returns his right to the ward, or if it is taken away from him because he has not fulfilled his obligations. Until its allocation, the free water right is held in trust by the ward representative. The rotation turns of this water right are sold to the water-right holders and the profits are used for the common good, such as the maintenance of the ward church.

Besides these free water rights, several wards have one or two water rights that are permanently managed by the ward. The irrigation turns of these water rights are usually given to the *mayordomo* of the ward, as compensation for the expenses he incurs as a result of his religious obligations.

The distribution of the water

The 192 water rights form the basis for the daily water distribution. The water-right holders receive their irrigation turns in an order determined by the ward in which they have their water rights: the water-right holders of the ward Santa Catarina get their turn first, followed by those of San Bernardino, La Asunción, La Magdalena, Santa Cruz Cuatla, San Martin Huaquechula and finally the water-right holders of Santa Cruz Tecoxco. The rotation then begins afresh with the water-right holders of Santa Catarina. Thus, the irrigation water is assigned to groups of people and not to groups of fields or tertiary blocks.

The duration of the rotation is determined as follows: simultaneously, four water-right holders receive their *cuarteron*, four times in succession, at six in the morning, at noon, six in the evening and at midnight. The time of the water application is defined by the specific water right. There are day water rights, with an irrigation rotation turn at six in the morning or at noon, and there are night water rights where the irrigation rotation starts at six in the evening or at midnight. In this way, 16 water-right holders can be supplied with water in any one day and night.

The turns work out as follows. First, the water-right holders from Santa Catarina receive their irrigation turn. This ward has 32 water rights, which implies that two days and two nights are needed. The same applies to the other wards that have 32 water rights: San Bernardino and La Asunción. One day and one night are sufficient for the three wards that have 16 water rights each. The 48 water-right holders of La Magdalena should, in principle, be able to get their water in three days and three nights. However, this ward has 32 night water rights and only 16 day water rights, which means that two days and four nights are necessary to supply water to all 48 water-right holders. The result is that the night rotation takes longer than the day rotation. Thirteen nights are needed for the night rotation (3 × 2 nights + 3 × 1 night + 1 × 4 nights) and 11 days for the day rotation (3 × 2 days + 3 × 1 day + 1 × 2 days). The day and the night rotations do not synchronize: the day and the night water-right holders of the ward usually do not get their irrigation turns on the same day.

Because the irrigation turns can be lent or sold, the distribution can be adjusted to individual needs. When a water-right holder needs water before his turn in the rotation, he will try to find someone whose turn is before his but is not going to use it. The latter can lend or sell his turn to the former. He may lend it if he expects to need water himself shortly: a water-right holder can ask to have his 'loaned' irrigation turn back at a later date, but he cannot buy back one that has been sold.

Furthermore, people without water rights can also buy irrigation turns. They may buy one turn, or several turns of one water right for a longer period, even up to several years. Most land owners who are not water-right holders obtain their water by negotiating share-farming agreements with the water-right holders. The former have land to offer, and the latter water. Most water-right holders disapprove of right-holders who sell water to farmers who own much land but do not have a water-right, but nonetheless this practice does occur. There is even a water-right holder who works permanently with a big land owner and buys water for him each day. Land owners who do not lease their land and only buy water are looked upon as antisocial by the right-holders because they deprive the landless right-holders of the chance to grow a crop.

The sale of water is also a delicate issue in the relationship between the wards and the government. Under Mexican law, the sale of water is illegal. This prohibition gives the big land owners an argument to push the government into imposing the law to ensure that the water is distributed in proportion to the land owned. However, there is no chance of this happening for the time being, first because the government departments in question lack the interest and the means, and secondly because a few big land owners have made themselves independent of the water-right holders by having wells dug on their land.

Water is distributed daily at the first division structure of the main canal. Usually, four times a day four water-right holders come to pick up their *cuarteron*. They discuss which plot each will take his water to and then adjust the division structure. This division structure is a concrete T-junction that splits the main canal into two. The distribution between these two canals is done roughly by placing a large metal sheet in one outlet. All four people who take a *cuarteron* are present when the plate is being positioned so that they witness the fair dividing up of the water.

When this has taken place, each leads his *cuarteron* to his plot by opening the division structures downstream. They consist of simple bifurcations. Some are made of concrete but most have no lining and are adjusted with stones, plastic and earth. Because the plots farmed by the irrigators are located all over the system, the water can be diverted to four other places every six hours. No particular person has the task of setting up the division structures or of supervising the water distribution. This is done by the water-right holders themselves, usually four times a day by four different water-right holders.

These four people are not the only individuals to be found at the first division structure. People with a right to an irrigation turn later in the day may arrive early to make arrangements for taking over a *cuarteron*. Because the system is large they look for someone who irrigates a plot close to theirs. In addition to water-right holders, people wishing to borrow or buy water also come to the first division structure. The first division structure is therefore a water market where the number of those present and the price of turns increase with the demand for irrigation water.

Irrigated farming

The fields are irrigated all year round to grow sugar-cane, maize, beans, vegetables and fruits. Cane now occupies about 30 per cent of the area. Ten years ago this percentage was even less; sugar-cane cultivation is increasing but has not yet matched the surrounding areas where almost 100 per cent is under cane. It is cultivated under contract and delivered to the sugar factory in Atencingo that offers cultivation loans, determines the harvesting time and takes care of the harvest and transport. On the west bank, cane is mostly grown on the land not owned by water-right holders. For the bigger land owners it is a lucrative crop that demands little labour or other inputs.

The water-right holders, whether or not they own land, choose different crops from the big land owners: beans and high-yielding varieties of maize. They sell part of the harvest and keep the other part to eat. Other important crops are rice (in the rainy season), onions, French beans, alfalfa and many vegetables and fruits. These crops are largely sold.

The fields are ploughed with hired tractors while teams of oxen make the furrows and do the weeding. The average plot size is 2 ha. Many fertilizers and chemical pesticides are used which are applied by hand. Sowing and harvesting are also done by hand.

Only one-quarter of the water-right holders of the western wards own one or more irrigable fields; most of the water-right holders own only the piece of *huerta* on which they live. They own only 30 per cent of the *barrio* fields, an average of 3.5 ha each. The remaining 70 per cent of the *barrio* fields is in the hands of non-*usuarios*. They each own an average of 8 ha, though two land owners own approximately 70 ha each.

On the east bank, at the time when, in 1966, the right to water became linked to land ownership, land was distributed more evenly. At the time of our research however, this property distribution seemed to have become less equitable. The average holding here is 2 ha and the biggest land owner owns about 20 ha. The difference between the eastern and the western wards is due partly to the fact that, in the 1920s and 1930s, Jenkins bought *barrio* ground only on the east bank and that later this land was excluded from the confines of the wards. On the west bank others (including water-right holders) bought land as well. This land, with larger farm sizes, still belongs to the territory of the western ward. According to one informant, some party-loving water-right holders have had to sell their land to pay their debts. Nowadays, many ward inhabitants have neither land nor a right to water. They work on the land as *peones* or have non-agricultural jobs.

Share farming (*medianía, cultivar a medias*) is common, particularly on the west bank. Here, land owner and share farmer each supply part of the means of production and split the yield equally between them (which explains the Spanish name). To land owners without a water right and without access to pumped-up groundwater, this is the most important way of getting water. Likewise, for water-right holders without land, share-farming is the most important strategy to obtain land for growing a crop. Linking the right to water to land ownership will have major repercussions on the lives of these almost landless water-right holders.

Principles of water distribution on the west bank

Now that we have described the water distribution and its context, we will examine a few of its features. These are derived from three questions about the right to water: where does one get one's right from, what are the benefits of a right, and what are the obligations that go with it.

Whether or not a person is given a water right is decided by the water-right holders as a group. When a water-right holder dies, his eldest son has first claim to the water right. The number of water-right holders remains constant. Each water-right holder receives an equal share of the total flow for a fixed period that is the same for all water-right holders.

A water-right holder must meet his religious obligations; these cost him time and money. Moreover, he has to spend time and money on main-tenance and on the irrigation board. The water-right holders of the western wards assume that the water is provided by the *barrio* saints and therefore willingly and dutifully serve these holy patrons who symbolize the unity of the community. The water belongs to the community; individuals who borrow water from the community must do something in return.

The water-right holders can be seen as the supporters of the religious organization in the ward. Because of the central position of the religious organization in the ward, the water-right holders play a key role in the functioning and survival of the ward as a religious unit. The organization of irrigation is not autonomous but is closely interwoven with the local society and is important for its functioning and survival.

Water allocation is ingrained in the organizational patterns of local society. When, in the beginning of this century, the communal fields of the wards started to pass into the hands of individuals, the allocation of the irrigation rights remained and became the most concrete manifestation of these patterns. The water allocation pattern slows down the spread of other patterns, such as further individualization, absorption into the market economy and into profit-oriented production, upscaling and modernization.

The structure of the water allocation and the religious organization tend to promote social equality. Each and every water-right holder has the right to an equal amount of water. When a well-to-do water-right holder organizes a religious feast, he is expected to spend more money than a water-right holder with fewer means. The richer water-right holders have more prestige. However, when the actual distribution takes place, certain mechanisms make the system flexible and allow inequality among the water-right holders. The rigidity of a fixed rotation sequence and a fixed rotation duration is overcome by exchanging turns. The amount of water is adjusted to the amount of land by share farming and by selling water. Ultimately, a water-right holder can get more water by representing the water-rights of others, usually family members who are absent or are no longer able to work with their *turno*.

To the technical eye of the westerner, who sees the daily distribution of water as a centralized process of distribution among plots of land, the daily water distribution appears to be complicated. The water users whose turn it is have a key role. There are no co-ordinating or controlling duties and there are few conflicts. Water division is regulated by an always changing group of individuals, according to clear rules that are known and accepted by all involved.

For the distribution of water among the seven western wards, each ward comprises an organizational irrigation unit of water users and not a territorial irrigation unit made up of a group of fields. There are two reasons for this. First, the seven western wards lie clustered together in a corner of the irrigated area. This makes it difficult to divide the irrigated area among the wards. In contrast, the eastern wards lie in a long row along the river with a strip of irrigated land running parallel. Here it is easier to divide the area with the fields into areas for each ward, and this is exactly what farmers did in 1966.

The second reason for the irrigation unit being a group of water users is the fact that there are water-right holders with very little land, or none, and land owners with hardly any right to water, or none. The water-right holders of a ward use their water right on plots that not only lie far apart but change each season, due to the changing share-farming relationships and the sale of water. The smallest territorial irrigation unit on the west bank is the entire irrigated area of the western wards, whereas on the east bank it is the ward.

Summary and conclusions

In Izúcar both irrigation and religion have pre-Columbian roots and until the 1930s they were organized in the same institutions. In 1934, the government introduced separate institutions for irrigation. These were assimilated into the organization of irrigation on both banks. Other processes after the intervention altered the organization on the east bank. In 1966, the government, in collaboration with a few farmers, linked the right to water to land ownership. This meant undoing the bond between irrigation and religion.

Irrigators on the west bank successfully resisted pressure from the government and by land owners without water rights to link water rights to land ownership. Because the water-right holders owned little or no land, they opposed this linkage. They succeeded because their resistance was fierce – they threatened the lives of government personnel – and because the government was divided by conflicts and had few means. Without the government behind them, the land owners without water rights were powerless against the resistance of the water-right holders.

Even though the share-farming contracts are in their favour, the land owners still try to become independent from the water of the water-right holders. This desire relates to the increase in sugar-cane cultivation. To the bigger land owners, sugar is a lucrative crop which they prefer to grow alone rather than with a share farmer, because sugar-cane requires little labour and few pesticides, the items supplied by the share farmer.

We view this process as the encroachment of economic patterns from outside the local community. In the past, the major land owners usually came from the wards; they firmly supported the traditional division of water and the system of share farming. Nowadays, most big land owners come from outside the wards or have broken away from the wards. These farmers follow a capitalist logic: they want to run their farming businesses alone and are less interested in share farming, because they want to maximize profit.

The land owners are trying to become independent from the water-right holders in two ways. First, they complain regularly to the government in the hope of getting its officers to link the right to water with land ownership. However, the government service responsible has neither the opportunity nor the will to do this. Second, in the course of the last decade, they have dug wells. The result is that the pressure on the holders of rights to change the water allocation has not increased.

The origin of a change in the distribution of water will not necessarily lie in the politico-economic struggle between water-right holders, land owners and government. The biggest threat to the distribution of water appears to be the fact that generation after generation, individual water-right holders, by their more intensive contact with 'modern life', will lose their ties with traditions, even if they keep their Catholic faith. At present, it appears that the importance of 'traditional' water distribution has slowed down this acculturation. A significant feature of irrigation organization on the west bank is that it is the water-right holders who decide whom they admit into their community. In this way they would seem to guarantee, to a large extent, the continuity of traditional society. A breakthrough would occur if the right to water became linked to land ownership: someone could then become a water-right holder by buying a piece of land, and the community would no longer have any influence over such a transaction. This change has taken place on the east bank. The circumstances and its effects on water division are discussed in the next chapter by Timen Eilander.

6. Rehabilitation of a farmer-managed system in Izúcar de Matamoros (east bank)

Two interpretations of technical concepts

TIMEN EILANDER[1]

Irrigation engineering's long-held views on planning and building systems have recently come to include rehabilitation, for two reasons: the systems constructed by the engineers are not working properly; there are fewer opportunities to set up new ones. Not only the systems constructed by engineers but also those built and managed by farmers are being rehabilitated. The rehabilitation usually entails rebuilding structures but may include changing the allocation and distribution of water. Engineers expect their interventions to improve the distribution of water in the long term; to them, this improvement usually means that water is used more efficiently. They usually try to raise efficiency by applying standard solutions, ignoring local principles of distribution and their background.

In this chapter I will examine a 1966 intervention by engineers in the indigenous irrigation system of the eastern wards of Izúcar de Matamoros, in Mexico. At the request of two farmers, the irrigation authority of the day, the Alto Balsas commission, linked the right to water to ownership of land. Before the intervention, the right to water was, as in the western wards, linked to individuals who in return had to serve the ward's saint. The commission withdrew from the eastern wards after a couple of months. In the wake of its departure the irrigators linked the right to water to land ownership in a manner that they fashioned themselves. This resulted in a new water distribution that consisted of both new and old elements.

The aim of this article is to compare the idea behind the water distribution plan developed by the commission's engineers with what the farmers have had in mind since 1966. These sets of ideas, which I will respectively refer to as the engineers' concept and the farmers' concept, consist of several principles of water distribution. I will discuss the differences between the two concepts and relate them to the differences in the context.

The eastern *barrios*

The wards lie in line from north to south along the east bank of the River Nexapa (see Figure 2 in Chapter 5). Each ward has a built-up area on the

[1] The author is a member of the Reformed Missionary Association (Gereformeerde Zendingsbond, GZB) and works in a church farming project in Peru. He collected the data for this chapter during his field research in the autumn of 1985.

Table 1: The eastern wards: order and area irrigated in 1966

Number	Name of the ward	Area (ha)
1	Santiago Mihuacan	269
2	San Diego	65
3	San Juan Piaxtla	80
4	San Juan Coahuixtla	35
5	Santo Tomas	22
6	Los Reyes	84
7	Santiago Mazatla	16

river levee where almost all houses as well as many orchards (*huertas*) are located. East of this old-established area lies the *campos*, clayey land reclaimed at the beginning of this century, on which few houses are built. Table 1 lists the wards from north to south and gives their number and the areas irrigated in 1966.

The system is similar to that of the western wards discussed in Chapter 5. The socio-economic and legal/administrative setting of the water distribution and irrigated farming is identical.

The engineers of the Alto Balsas commission and their water distribution plan

The central government set up the Alto Balsas commission in 1960. Its main task was to coordinate the policy of the departmental irrigation services in the upper part of the catchment area of the River Balsas, of which the Nexapa is a part. In addition, the commission was entrusted with enforcing an irrigation law, stipulating that access to water must be proportional to land ownership. Its office was established in Izúcar.

In 1966, the commission set up a water distribution plan to implement a water distribution regulation requested by two farmers from ward 1. Engineers working for the commission asked the farmers to produce the dimensions of their plots in square metres. They drew up a list in which they arranged the plots per canal and combined plots lying along one canal to form basic units within which the water rotation took place. The area of the basic units varied from 10 to 100 ha. Next, the engineers allocated a flow of 0.64 l/s/ha to each basic unit. (During the field research, the farmers referred to this as 1 l/s/ha.) They fixed the rotation interval at one week, calculated the time allotted to each plot with a precision of ten minutes and fixed the order of rotation within the list.

In the plan, the distribution of water between the units was proportional to the area of the farmer's land. The engineers constructed proportional division structures in the larger canals. The width of the branches of each structure corresponded to the areas lying behind them. These division structures were not built in the smaller canals, probably due to lack of funds.

The most important allocation principles are listed below:

- Water rights are linked to land ownership.
- Water rights are obtainable only through the purchase or inheritance of land.
- Irrigation time is proportionate to land owned and calculated in units of ten minutes.
- The area that can be supplied with water from one canal is the basic distribution unit.
- Within the basic unit, water rotation takes place in a fixed order and the duration of the rotation is constant.

The engineers' context

The context of the engineers' concept can be divided into two parts: that of the government or administration employing the engineers; and that of the engineer as technician. At the government level, the reason to make the right to water proportional to land owned is its policy of increasing national agricultural production. The government believes that a farmer will be able to produce most if the allocation of water is linked to the allocation of land, because it assumes that in this manner water will be distributed as efficiently as possible. Underlying this policy is the socio-economic motive of feeding the growing population. In addition, the legislation on irrigation rights increases the government's hold on the farmer-managed irrigation systems.

The policy of increasing agricultural production by linking the right to water to the area of land owned is determined culturally, as it is part of western culture. The concepts of efficiency and optimization are important in western agricultural science and indeed to the entire western way of thinking. In this ideology, a farmer is an entrepreneur striving to achieve the highest yield at the lowest cost. This cultural aspect is found in other political measures to raise agricultural production; the Mexican government promotes large-scale farming, specialization in a limited number of crops and the use of high-yielding varieties. The commission's engineers try to achieve these targets.

Let us now consider the second element in the engineers' context: the engineer as technician. How have the engineers expressed the link between the right to water and land ownership in terms of their water distribution plan? By applying this link literally, they have tried to set down precisely how much water goes to which plot and when. This enables them to fix the rotation period and the order of rotation.

The quantitative approach in this water distribution plan is striking.

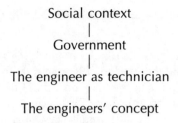

Figure 1 *Model of the engineers' context that determines the engineers' concept*

Actually, this method is used often in western science and technology. By expressing the facts in figures and by systematically simplifying them, they become more orderly and easier to grasp.

The simplification depends on the context. The engineers assume in their plan that there is a single cropping pattern. There is no room for any variation of crops. This corresponds with their belief that the increase in production must be brought about by specialization, thus by monoculture. This is outlined schematically in Figure 1. The government's socio-economic motive for increasing agricultural production, and the cultural choices made by the government and the engineers can be described as the impact of the social context.

The farmers' problems with the engineers' plan

The engineers' water distribution plan met with resistance from the farmers. Their objections were clear and simple. Nobody can irrigate with a precision of exactly ten minutes. Moreover, big farmers in small units needed to spend more time on irrigation because the flow was less than before 1966. For example, consider a farmer with 1.5 ha in a basic unit of 10.5 ha. He received a weekly flow of 6.5 l/s for a duration of 24 hours. Before 1966 he got 50 to 60 l/s. In contrast, a farmer with 0.15 ha in a basic unit of 80 ha got only 20 minutes of water. To water the root zone adequately, the water needed to flow across the field for a much longer time.

The older farmers told me that the water distribution plan of the engineers was operational for only a few months. The farmers quickly switched to a new method of water division that they devised themselves. This switch coincided with the dissolution of the Alto Balsas commission. Interestingly, the farmers do not object to the division structures in the larger canals, possibly because they allow the farmers to see how the water is divided.

The farmers and the water distribution on the east bank before 1966

On the east bank water was distributed in much the same way before 1966 as it is on the west bank today. Until 1966 the right to water meant the duty to fulfil religious obligations for the patron saint of the ward, besides the duties of the irrigation organization. Each water-right holder in the ward had the right to one turn (*turno*) which was equal to a water right of 12 hours and was obtained through inheritance.

There were, however, a few differences that made it easier to link the right to water to land ownership. Unlike in the western wards, the number of water-right holders was not restricted. Residents of the ward who put in a request for water were allocated a right to water by the group of water-right holders. Every ward resident could obtain a right to water if he was male, older than 18 years and willing to take on the religious and non-religious obligations that accompanied the status of water-right holder. Thus, when 18, the sons of the bigger farmers were able to get turns for their fathers' lands which could be used to irrigate even more land.

A second difference between the east bank before 1966 and the west bank was that on the east bank each ward operated as a basic unit. Water was rotated between the water-right holders in this unit. The total flow was first divided between the seven wards, each of which received a *surco* (portion of water) of about 65 l/s at the beginning of the dry season. The biggest ward (number 1) received two *surcos*. At the moment their turn came, water-right holders would collect these eight *surcos* at the inlet of the eastern wards, at six in the morning or at six in the evening. In contrast, the seven wards on the west bank together formed one basic unit.

Since the right to water was not linked to the ownership of land, one should view the ward as a group of people and not as a number of contiguous fields. An outsider might be tempted to adopt the latter view, because each ward had an area where most of the parcels belonging to the water-right holders were situated. Each water-right holder possessed the right to transfer his turn to a plot in another ward or to a field of a non-*usuario* inside or outside his ward. Consequently, the pattern of distribution over the canals and the main canals must have changed daily. Besides, there were no fixed division structures in the canal system on the east bank.

A third difference was that the water-right holders on the east bank did not all use the same distribution procedures. The water-right holders of the three northern wards divided up the water for their ward differently from the irrigators in the four southern wards. In the three northern wards, each water-right holder had to apply to a *repartidor* (divider of the water) to get his turn. This *repartidor* was a water-right holder too. In the four southern wards the order of the turns was fixed, so each water-right holder knew when he had his turn. This split between the eastern wards corresponds with another social dichotomy: the inhabitants of the three northern wards married among themselves, as did the inhabitants of the four southern wards.

The most important allocation principles that were in force on the east bank prior to 1966 are listed below:

• The right to water is linked to the fulfilment of religious duties.
• The right to water is obtained through a decision of the group of water-right holders or through inheritance.
• Each water-right holder is entitled to one turn.
• The basic unit is the ward, which consists of a group of people.
• In the three northern wards, a *repartidor* divides the water upon request; in the four southern wards, water is distributed in a fixed order and according to a rotation with a constant duration.

Water distribution after 1966

After the engineers' plan failed, the farmers modified their previous water distribution method. It came to consist of many features of the water distribution practised before 1966 but also included some innovations, such as the link between the right to water and land ownership.

The farmers reinstated the basic distribution units in the wards, but had to determine which plots belonged to which ward because they maintained the link between the right to water and land ownership. The concept of ward came to mean a group of contiguous fields. In most cases the farmers used the administrative borders of the ward, as these were also territories with a representative in the municipal government. In this way it could happen that plots situated along one canal were assigned to different wards, whereas the engineers allocated all parcels on a canal to a same basic unit. The farmers split ward number 1 that had two *surcos* before 1966 into two basic units, with each unit receiving half the flow. However, at the administrative level of the irrigation board that manages the seven wards, ward 1 kept its status of a single ward. This illustrates that even after 1966, the concept *barrio*, meaning a community of people, remained relevant.

The farmers also retained the principle of basing the allocation of water on the area of the wards. In places where the engineers constructed proportional division structures, water is still distributed proportionally to the areas behind. Where there is no division structure, the farmers divide the water between the wards roughly in proportion to the areas of the wards. The water allocation to wards 3, 4 and 5, whose areas comprise 80, 35 and 22 ha respectively, is 2:1:1. This division is similar to the division into *surcos* that the farmers employed before 1966.

The farmers maintained the pre-1966 distinction between three northern and four southern wards. Since 1966, the farmers in the three northern wards have had to apply to a *repartidor* for their water, who gives them a quota (which can be expressed in h/ha). The amount depends on the flow that is available but always satisfies the needs of the crop. The farmers call this form of irrigation *riego por terminado*, which means 'irrigate until you have finished'. In the four southern wards the farmers irrigate according to *riego por turnos*, which literally means 'irrigation per rotation turn'. In farming terms, a *turno* implies a turn of 12 hours. This form of irrigation has a fixed rotation order and a fixed duration, irrespective of the crop and the flow available.

Riego por terminado

Under the *riego por terminado* method a farmer gets a quota of water that depends on the crop grown and on the water in the canals. It is based on experience and not set down in writing. Only some farmers are capable of expressing it in h/ha. All know, however, how many 12-hour turns are needed for a field with a particular crop.

The quota and rotation durations for the various crops show differences that are both logical and significant (see Table 2). To allow a comparison, I have calculated an irrigation application and a monthly total based on the flow at the start of the dry season.

Table 2 shows that the farmers adjust the quota and the rotation duration to the needs of the crops. They strive to water the crop adequately at each turn. After the rainy season, the decrease in flow is counterbalanced by an increase in the quota. 'Less water, more hours' plays an important role in the farmer's interpretation. Increasing the quota means lengthening the duration of the rotation. It often takes up to 20 days and may even last one month. If a farmer asks his *repartidor* for water when the dry season has just started, he can have it on the following day, if he asks for water when the dry season is almost over, he may have to wait almost one week. The lengthening rotation duration threatens the drought-susceptible crops.

This manner of distributing water can function properly only if the

Table 2: The quota and the rotation duration of five crops at the start of the dry season

Crop	h/ha	mm	rotation duration	mm/month
Huerta	4	100	22–24 days	150
Papalo[1]	4	100	7–8 days	400
Beans	6	150	10 days	450
Maize	6	150	12 days	375
Alfalfa	8	200	15–20 days	356

[1] *Papalo* is a vegetable.

repartidor may be trusted by the irrigators. This requirement helps explain why the farmers chose the wards as their basic distribution units. By linking irrigation organization and residential units, they give themselves additional means for controlling the water divider.

There are of course limits to ward size. In most wards there are between 20 and 30 water-right holders, but the largest ward, number 1, has about 150 farmers. In this ward, the farmers are divided into six groups of 20 to 30 water-right holders, irrespective of how much land they own.

The allocation and distribution principles of *riego por terminado* are summarized below:

- The right to water is linked to land owned.
- The right to water is either bought or inherited.
- Water is distributed through a *repartidor* who divides according to the needs of the crop and pro rata the land area.
- The ward is the basic distribution unit.
- Water is supplied on request.

The farmers' context
The context in which water is allocated may be viewed from two perspectives. One is the water users as a group. Before 1966, the nature of this group was determined by the link between water and religion. *Barrio* water was distributed on the basis of one turn per water-right holder. Social equality was paramount in this distribution: an adult resident of the ward merely needed to fulfil his religious obligations to obtain rights to water. Consequently, every member of the ward community could obtain a supply of water. Anyone who wished to fulfil his religious obligations in the ward church was ensured of a turn. Under the present water distribution system, it is solely membership of the ward community that entitles the farmers to their share of the water.

The second perspective is the farmer and his crop. Before starting to grow a crop, a farmer wants to know if he will be assured of enough water for the whole growing season and whether he will be able to get water when he needs it. This implies that the supply of water should be geared to the specific needs of one or more crops.

These two considerations together determine which allocation concept and which accompanying distribution rules a farmer favours. It seems that the socio-economic context affects his preference through the aspect 'farmer and crop'. These relationships are sketched in Figure 2.

Prior to 1966, a farmer had several options to modify his turn to the water needs of his crops. Some of these, such as exchanging turns and share cropping, can still be seen in the western wards. Secondly, since the number of water-right holders in the eastern wards was not limited, the bigger farmers with sons older than 18 received an extra turn. Thirdly, in

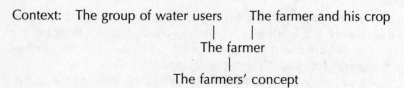

Figure 2 *Model of the farmers' context that determines the farmers' concept*

the three northern wards the principle of 'turns on request' was applied. In these ways, the farmers translated their allocation into a distribution that met the water requirements of their crops.

Before 1966, the water was distributed according to the concept *turno*. To the farmers, this concept encompassed the relationship with the ward and the equality of the water-right holders. This allocation principle corresponded with the concept of 'group of water users'. To gear their turns to the needs of their crops, the farmers could swap their *turnos*. This notion of 'the farmer and his crop' was expressed only informally, through exchange of turns and not through the formal allocation principles in use before 1966.

In 1966 the decision to keep the ward as the basic unit affected the outlook of the group of water users. In that year, although the ward became a group of contiguous fields, the decision to use the ward as basic unit allowed the water users to link up with local institutions. The farmers believed that this helped bring about an effective water distribution.

The request to link the right to water to the ownership of land was made by two big farmers in ward 1. In 1966, farmers in this ward owned twice as much land as they could irrigate with their water rights. Big farmers with more land than water rights suffered most from the shortage of water in their ward, as it prevented them from growing lucrative crops. They may also have been unsure whether the supply would be enough to water the crop until the end of the growing season. By contrast, other wards had a surplus of water, which the water-right holders sold to people outside the ward.

The change in the concept by the two big farmers in ward 1 is only partly explained by the shortage of water in that ward. Their thinking was also affected by the changes triggered by the arrival of Jenkins (see Chapter 5). His entrepreneurship increased the emphasis on producing for the market. Many smaller farmers from ward 1 and all irrigators from the other wards had no problem in getting sufficient water from the water distribution system that existed before 1966. For them there was no reason to link water rights to land ownership.

In the current *riego por turnos*, the division of water between the water-right holders is still paramount, but the equality between the water-right holders has disappeared. Since 1966, a water-right holder has had the right to one or more turns in proportion to the land he owns. This can be seen in the actual distribution. The farmers gear these turns to the needs of their crops, by exchanging surpluses.

In the current *riego por terminado* the farmers use the concept *turno* as a measure to tune the water gift to the needs of the crop. Since 1966, the meaning of the concept 'turn' has altered in favour of the farmer and his crop, to allow an allocation that is directly geared to the needs of the crop.

Comparisons and conclusions

The water allocation concepts of the engineers and the farmers are at odds in many respects. The differences can be traced to differences in the contexts of both groups. The engineers considered only the physical aspects of water distribution. In their eyes, the division of water is best guaranteed if it is clear how much water goes to which plot and when. For the farmers, their share of the water is best guaranteed if the group of water users joins up with the local ward community.

In their allocation plan, the engineers ignored the context in which the irrigation system was embedded. They arrived at a concept in which the criteria are almost inseparably interconnected: linking the right to water to the ownership of land implies a fixed rotation duration, a fixed order and a basic unit consisting of the plots and one canal. Such fixed linkages are unthinkable to the farmers. They tied the right to water solely to land ownership, to gear the water distribution to the needs of the crops. Their preference for using the wards as the basic distribution units together with the concept of 'the farmer and his crop' determined which principles of allocation they chose. They tied water rights to land owned without radically changing other components of their allocation and distribution. Rather, they modified the meaning of the concepts *barrio* and *turno* somewhat but did not discard them.

The differences between the concepts of the engineers and the farmers also explain the accuracy with which the engineers calculated the water allocation. The precision in their calculations refers to a desire to control water distribution and to apply the linkage of water rights to land owner-ship. The farmers applied this 'linkage' less literally and not so accurately, so that it had little effect on the other components of the allocation and distribution. Greater accuracy in the distribution of water seems associated with strong linkages between the various criteria and less flexibility in the relationships between the farmer, his crop and the local context.

Both the engineers and the farmers strive to achieve the highest possible production but have different ideas on the implications for water manage-ment. The farmers believe that the *certainty* of a right to water and *gearing* the allocated water to the needs of their crops are most important. As members of a group of water users who have to share the scarce water, they have to use the water efficiently. In the eyes of the engineers of the commission the concept of *efficiency* is paramount. By strictly linking the water right to land ownership, not a drop of water needs to be wasted. In this way, all the farmers of the eastern wards will achieve maximum production. Although the engineers and the farmers have comparable objectives, they arrive at totally different water distribution concepts because of their different points of departure.

The basic unit of the engineers closely corresponds to the tertiary block in a large irrigation scheme: a group of contiguous fields, watered from a common canal that is fed by an inlet point in the secondary network. The application of this tertiary block idea creates tension with the water allocation concepts of the farmers. The basic unit they have chosen shows that the farmers consider that forming a close-knit group of water users is more important. For reasons of social control this group should be part of the local community and not exceed a certain size. The division of the 150 irrigators in ward 1 into six groups indicates that 20 to 30 farmers per group is the maximum, at least in the situation of Izúcar.

The decision of the engineers to take one canal as the basic unit deprived the farmers of the opportunity to gear the water application to the needs of their crops. By taking the ward as the basic unit, the farmers control the flow so that they are able to irrigate their crops properly without wasting much water or time. The division of the large flow of ward 1 into two equal parts shows that the farmers prefer a flow that they can manage. In the eastern wards this flow is approximately 60 l/s.

In western irrigation technology, plant/water relationships are important. With this relationship, a crop and a manageable flow of 40 l/s in mind, an engineer calculates the optimum duration of one application of water. Then, on the basis of the optimum rotation duration and the optimum plot size he calculates the optimum size of a tertiary block. No such calculation model can be traced in the rehabilitation of the engineers of the Alto Balsas commission. All those engineers did was divide the flow by the surface area, to arrive at a quota of 0.64 l/s/ha. Using this quota, they calculated the inlet flow of the basic units, which they had determined according to the situation of the canals.

As engineers, we must not only be aware that this type of calculation is based on *efficiency* but must also question whether this way of designing a water distribution system is suitable in the rehabilitation of a farmer-managed system. In Izúcar de Matamoros, the engineer is confronted with a canal system that does not fit the concept of the optimum size of a tertiary block nor the corresponding calculation model because that concept assumes that a tertiary block is a group of contiguous fields instead of a group of water-right holders.

7. From allocation to distribution

Operational rules in a communal irrigation system in Northern Portugal

PAUL HOOGENDAM, ADRI VAN DEN DRIES, JOSÉ PORTELA, MONIEK STAM and JULIA CARVALHO[1]

Irrigation is important in all agrarian villages in the region of Trás-os-Montes in Northern Portugal. Water from different sources protects meadows against freezing during the winter and complements water deficits in the production of food crops in the summer. The irrigation practices in 42 Trás-os-Montes villages have recently been studied.[2] The research focused mainly on the communal irrigation systems, which are owned and used by the largest number of water users in the area and which are all operated on the basis of detailed agreements for the allocation of water. Several principles for allocation were encountered (see Chapter 8, which also discusses irrigation in Northern Portugal). In all systems, the allocation of water forms the basis for water distribution within the systems.

Detailed allocation of water alone does not achieve distribution. Operational rules are necessary, to convert abstract water rights into actual discharges and flow to chosen parts of the irrigation area during determined periods of time. In this article we present the rules that the water users of Vila Cova, one of the Trás-os-Montes villages, have created to distribute the water in accordance with the allocation. We will also analyse the extent to which these rules enable the water users to turn their rights into real flows.

In the international literature, little mention is made of the conversion of water rights into day-to-day water distribution. It may be implicitly assumed that water allocation is linearly translated into flows; in practice, this seldom occurs. The conversion of rights into distribution is often a complex process and may transform a fair allocation into an unfair

[1] Paul Hoogendam is lecturer at Wageningen Agricultural University (WAU), Department of Irrigation and Soil and Water Conservation, Wageningen, The Netherlands; Adri van den Dries is irrigation researcher in Trás-os-Montes; José Portela is Professor of Rural Sociology at the Universidade de Trás-os-Montes e Alto Douro (UTAD), Vila Real, Portugal. Moniek Stam, student at WAU, and Julia Carvalho, student at UTAD, did field research in Vila Cova in the summer of 1992. The authors express their appreciation to Geert Diemer for his valuable comments on an earlier draft of this paper.
[2] These studies were undertaken within the framework of a joint research programme of the Department of Irrigation and Soil and Water Conservation at WAU and the Department of Economics and Sociology at UTAD (Bleumink and Kuik 1992). This article is based on a four-month case study on the functioning of the communal irrigation system in the village of Vila Cova (Stam 1993). Complementary information on specific points was obtained through later interviews with key informants.

distribution. The rules that the irrigators have developed in Vila Cova provide the water users with fairly equal opportunities to obtain the water to which they are entitled. These rules are context-specific but may serve as a basis for creative ideas about operational rules in other systems.

We will begin by presenting the history and details of contemporary water allocation in Vila Cova.

The village of Vila Cova

Physical and socio-economic environment

Vila Cova is a mountain community of farming households in Trás-os-Montes. The village lies 17 km from Vila Real, the main city of the region (see Figure 1) on the edge of the mountain chain of Alvão, at 750 m above sea level. The climate is harsh, with cold, wet winters and hot, dry summers. Average yearly rainfall amounts to 1870 mm, of which 85 per cent falls between October and March. Crop growth is constrained by low temperatures in spring, risk of frosts in the crop-growing season and a moisture deficit in the summer.

Vila Cova is inhabited by 250 people, who belong to 100 households. At least 40 of the 150 houses in Vila Cova belong to emigrants who only occupy them in August, during their summer holidays. The social infra-

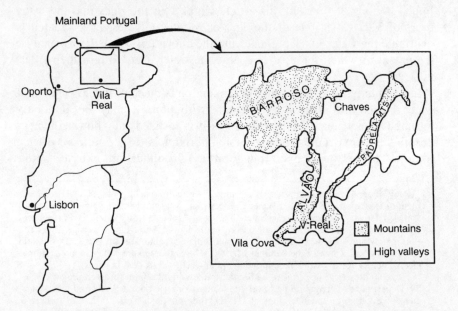

Figure 1 *Location of Vila Cova*

structure includes a chapel, a church, a primary school (seven pupils in 1992), and three small shops/cafes. Electricity and tap water are present. Public matters are handled by the Village Council. Social life in Vila Cova is informal. Family ties are the most important social relations. Exchanges of resources, particularly of labour, between neighbours are also crucial.

Vila Cova prospered between 1940 and 1960, when mining of iron ore was an important source of income. Its population nearly doubled, houses were built and rented out and all agricultural production was consumed and sold locally. The closure of the mines and the fall of prices for agricultural products brought about the village economic decline. Since 1960, many farmers have emigrated to Portuguese cities and neighbouring countries. The population has diminished to less than half, and today nearly every family has a relative working abroad. The result is an ageing resident population, with pensioners older than 65 years representing nearly 40 per cent of the inhabitants. Only a quarter of the households are engaged in full-time farming. The others combine farming with off-farm activities. Nevertheless, agricultural production remains an essential part of the income of most families.

Agriculture
The households in Vila Cova own small landholdings, which comprise many small, scattered plots. Currently, agriculture is constrained by lack of labour. Production processes continue to be labour-intensive although many household members have left the village. Therefore, elderly people and children contribute to daily chores and household members engaged in off-farm work usually help on Saturdays and during holidays. Mechanization is increasing gradually. In peak periods, additional labour is mobilized through exchanges with neighbours and family members. Other resources are also obtained through such exchanges.

Farming in Vila Cova has hardly specialized. All families cultivate potatoes, maize and vegetables, mainly for home consumption. Some farmers gain additional income by raising cattle for milk and/or meat, but the average herd is only two animals. Animal feeding is based on meadows for green fodder, grazing and hay. Only one farmer owns a flock of sheep which he usually grazes on the communal lands. The communal lands also supply firewood and material for cattle bedding.

Winter and summer irrigation and the communal irrigation system

All water sources are exploited for agricultural purposes, even those with flows of less than 1 l/s. The most important water source is the river that passes through the village, the *Ribeiro de Vila Cova*. Although its flow decreases considerably when summer advances, it is the main source for summer irrigation water. Other sources are springs, galleries and shallow and deep wells. These are owned and used individually or by small groups. The river water irrigates the main part of the cultivated land of the village by means of a collective irrigation system. The rules governing the conversion of water allocation into actual distribution are the main subject of this article.

Irrigated agriculture is divided into winter and summer irrigation. During these periods the area irrigated, allocation arrangements and distribution rules differ. In winter the arrangements are rather loose, since water greatly exceeds demand. In summer, arrangements are strict, since scarcity of water and increased crop water requirements lead to greater competition for water.

Winter irrigation: from October until June
In the winter period, most river water is used on permanent natural meadows on the slopes of the river valley. The meadows produce hay and are grazed after the hay harvest. Winter irrigation prevents the grass from freezing and speeds up re-growth in spring. The wet conditions may also regulate the composition of plant species in the pasture (Gonçalves 1985). Most meadows are situated upstream of the village and of the main intake that supplies the irrigated *veiga* (see below). Brushwood dams convey the water into earthen canals, which spill over to the adjacent meadows. These irrigation facilities are owned and maintained by small groups or by individual water users.

During the winter, access to water is free: all villagers may use the water where and whenever they want. Agreements between the water users are made only when the flow diminishes. Nevertheless, the basic rule of 'first come, first served' is applied: as long as a water user is irrigating his field, he must be respected; consequently, the water may not be diverted by others.

Summer irrigation: from the end of June until the end of September
During the summer, water is mainly applied to food crops cultivated primarily for household needs. Some water is used for the cultivation of cattle feed (meadows for green pasture, green maize etc.). The demand for water increases during the summer, since crop water needs increase and the rainfall diminishes.

The principal summer irrigation area is the *veiga*, a flat area of heavily manured, good quality soils located near the village. Its 60 ha are divided into about 260 plots with an average size of 0.23 ha. Plots in the *veiga* are intensively used for food crops (potatoes and maize) in summer (April–September) and as pasture in the winter (October–April). The irrigation water for the area is obtained from the communal irrigation system of Vila Cova.

The communal irrigation system

The system that serves the *veiga* is called the communal irrigation system, since 82 of the 100 Vila Cova households have access to the water of this system. Its name means 'People's Irrigation Canal'. Figure 2 shows the communal irrigation system and the present and former landholdings (*casais*) that it includes. The system comprises a permanent diversion structure in the Vila Cova river, a conveyance canal 50 m long, which bifurcates into two primary canals that split downstream into various branches, totalling about 3500 m. The system mainly serves the *veiga*. Water users extract the irrigation water directly from these canals or convey it through a network of field channels. The operation of the communal system is subject to detailed rights, rules and regulations that are the outcome of historical processes. These will be discussed below.

Water allocation in the communal irrigation system

The origin of the actual water allocation dates back to the time that the *veiga* was the property of nine *casais* (plural of *casal*), homesteads of extended families cultivating defined areas of land. In a collective effort, the *casais* created the infrastructure to irrigate their landholdings. It is no longer remembered when and how this was done. From the actual allocation it may be hypothesized that from the outset every *casal* obtained a time share of water and that a mono-flux rotation among the *casais* was established. This rotation lasted 11 days: eight of the nine *casais* were allowed to use the whole water flow for 24 hours, the ninth *casal* was entitled to use it for three days. The days of the rotation were named after the respective *casais*. The distribution within the *casal* landholding was not further prescribed; the water could be used according to the desire of the family holding the water rights.

Current allocation is based on this historical foundation and consists of two levels. The first level corresponds to the original rotation among *casais*. The days of the rotation still bear the names of the historical *casais* or the cultivated areas that they owned although the three-day period of the ninth *casal* has been divided into separate days. The second level refers to the allocation within every *casal* day. The 24 hours have been fragmented into smaller time shares belonging to different water users.

This fragmentation largely coincided with the fragmentation of the landholdings that occurred as a consequence of inheritance, buying and selling, marriages, etc. With every division of land, the water right related to the land was also divided into smaller portions. Water rights have also been exchanged, bought, and sold, and this has blurred the formerly clear-cut water allocation.

The result of the fragmentation is that most farmers have plots and

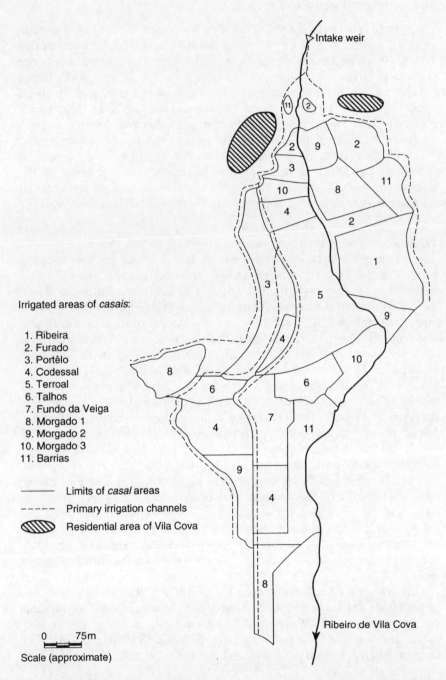

Intake weir

Irrigated areas of *casais*:

1. Ribeira
2. Furado
3. Portêlo
4. Codessal
5. Terroal
6. Talhos
7. Fundo da Veiga
8. Morgado 1
9. Morgado 2
10. Morgado 3
11. Barrias

——— Limits of *casal* areas

- - - - - Primary irrigation channels

▨ Residential area of Vila Cova

Ribeiro de Vila Cova

0   75m

Scale (approximate)

Figure 2 *The communal irrigation system and its irrigated area* (veiga)

attached water rights in several historical *casal* landholdings. However much these rights may have been fragmented, each right remains defined in terms of the time that the whole water flow may be used and in terms of its place in the *casal* allocation sequence.[3] These time shares vary from a few minutes to several hours. Accumulated access to water varies greatly among the water users: some users have access to several minutes only, whereas a few others total up over ten hours of water right.

All time shares and their order are written down in an allocation schedule. The most recent water allocation schedule dates back to 1968 and is in the possession of the president of the Village Council and a small number of farmers. Table 1 shows a transcript of the water schedule of *casal* Portêlo.

The water schedule is far from accurate. It gives names of right holders who are no longer active water users, and time shares do not always correspond with the present allocation of irrigation water. During the irrigation season of 1992, however, these deficiencies gave rise to few doubts or comments about the water rights.

Water distribution: rules and actions to implement water rights

The allocation of time shares forms the basis of the distribution of water among the users but it is not easy to transform an allocation into a distribution. The management of water flows raises its own questions, such as what to do with water losses in canals, how to cope with the travel time of water, what sequence of users to follow, and how to distribute night turns. These issues can be solved only through arrangements. In Vila Cova it is felt that these arrangements should provide all water users with equal opportunities to obtain the share of water to which they are entitled, and that they should prevent disagreements among the users.

The system of Vila Cova has elaborate rules that govern the day-to-day operation of the system. These rules contain much detail and address a variety of questions.

Beginning and ending the summer irrigation period
The beginning and end of the summer period are important dates, since water distribution is strictly arranged only during this period. Officially, the summer period starts on 24 June, the feast of Saint John. In practice, however, the season starts when water users feel that they have to wait

---

[3] Whether an irrigator uses the whole flow depends mainly on its size (*main d'eau*). If it is too large to handle, arrangements between neighbours may be necessary to divide it and to lengthen the irrigation time.

Table 1: The water allocation schedule

The third *casal*, Portêlo, begins in Ovelheira, goes on to Portêlo and ends in Tapado.

Place	Name of user	minutes
Ovelheira	Cândida Duro	42
	Maria Emília da Fonte	42
	Delfina Duro	7
Portêlo	José Manuel Duro	68
	América de Barros	12
	Amélia Duro	8
	José Pereira	119
	Delfina Duro	53
	Manuel Joaquim Carvalho Duro	25
	Joaquim Alves	18
	António Farroco	18
	Filomena Farroco	50
	Januário da Fonte	30
	Ana Pereira	24
	Conceiçao Pereira	23
	António Martins Ondas	23
	Ermelinda Duro	5
	Manuel Conçalves	5
	Teresa Lourenço	35
	Joaquim Carvalho	30
	Manuel Joaquim Duro	15
	Joaquim Gravelos	7
	António Martins Ondas	57
	Januário da Fonte	30
	António Pereira Gouvinhas	13
Tapado	Manuel Augusto Moreira	130
	Francisco Freixieira	5
	Joaquim Carvalho	6
	Joaquim Carvalho	40
	Belarmino Ramalho	30
	Joaquim Alves	18
	José Manuel Duro	34
	Joaquim Gravelos	15
	Joao Pereira Vasconcelos	31
	Florinda Pires	60
	Amérrica Calado	43
	Manuel Augusto Moreira	51
TOTAL		1342

This *casal* has water for 22 hours and 22 minutes and includes a travel time of water of 1 hour and 38 minutes.

too long under the 'first come, first served' rule. They start to pressure the Village Council to apply the summer irrigation schedule.

This practice makes the date to start summer irrigation flexible. In 1992, for instance, it was decided to postpone summer irrigation until 29 June, since water was still abundant due to showers in the first three weeks of that month. The summer period may also start before the official date. When this happens, the meadows upstream of the intake of the communal system may still be irrigated until 24 June. The date of the last day of the official summer period, 29 September, the feast of Saint Michael, is also flexible. When rains appear early in September, the summer distribution is gradually abandoned before the end of the month.

Deciding which group starts the summer irrigation

Two Sundays before 24 June the priest announces in church that the next Sunday, after mass, it will be decided where that year's irrigation will start. For this purpose, the *casais* are divided into two fixed groups, named *Veiga* (seven *casais*) and *Morgado* (four *casais*). To decide which group may start off using the water, the president of the Village Council invites someone to draw one of two straws representing the two groups. The group represented by the straw drawn may start to irrigate.

Deciding the sequence of the casais in the groups

Within the two groups agreements exist about the order of the *casais*. In the *Morgado* group this sequence is fixed: *Morgado 1, 2* and *3* and then *Barrias*. In the *Veiga* group the sequence changes between odd and even years. In even years the sequence is roughly from the *casais* at the head end of the group to the *casais* at the tail end (from upstream to downstream, in the direction of the canal flow). In odd years the sequence is reversed.

The sequences that are feasible may be found by combining the group that starts with the order of *casais* in the groups. This shows that four sequences are possible (Table 2).

The start of the casal day

Once it has been decided which group will start the summer irrigation, a clock is put in a window of the priest's house in the centre of the village. The time shown on this clock is 1.5 hours behind the official time.[4] This difference stems from former days when a sun clock, attached to one of the houses, indicated the irrigation time. In 1957, this house and its sun clock were destroyed. Two months later a clock was purchased, which was set at the same time as indicated formerly by the sun clock. To date, the irrigation day of every *casal* has started around sunrise, at 04.00 h irrigation time

---

[4] In 1993, it lagged behind 2.5 hours, since summer time was introduced in Portugal.

Table 2: Possible sequences of *casal* irrigation days

YEAR	EVEN straw 1	EVEN straw 2*	UNEVEN straw 1	UNEVEN straw 2
DAY	Veiga	Morgado	Veiga	Morgado
1	Ribeira	Morgado 1	Fundo da Veiga	Morgado 1
2	Furado	Morgado 2	Talhos	Morgado 2
3	Portêlo	Morgado 3	Terroal	Morgado 3
4	Codessal	Barrias	Codessal	Barrias
5	Terroal	Ribeira	Portêlo	Fundo da Veiga
6	Talhos	Furado	Furado	Talhos
7	Fundo da Veiga	Portêlo	Ribeira	Terroal
8	Morgado 1	Codessal	Morgado 1	Codessal
9	Morgado 2	Terroal	Morgado 2	Portêlo
10	Morgado 3	Talhos	Morgado 3	Furado
11	Barrias	Fundo da Veiga	Barrias	Ribeira

* In 1992 the straw of Morgado was drawn. Since it was an even year, sequence number two was followed.

(05.30 h official time). The next morning at the same hour the water flow is taken over by water users from the next *casal*.

The irrigation sequence within a casal

The sequence of water users within a *casal* changes with the irrigation turn of the *casal*. The idea is to avoid having the same water users always receiving their turn at night or at the end of the day. The irrigation turn of every *casal* is divided into three eight-hour parts and the water users of the *casal* are divided into three sub-groups. The order of these groups changes with every *casal* turn. For simplicity's sake we may call these groups A (upstream, water users 'a' to 'g'), B (middle, users 'h' to 'p') and C (downstream, users 'q' to 'z'). One in every three turns each sub-group has to irrigate at night. Therefore three sequences between the sub-groups are established (see Table 3).

The first sequence follows the water from upstream to downstream (A–B–C; from user 'a' to user 'z'). The second sequence takes place in the opposite direction, from the last to the first water user (C–B–A; 'z'–'a'). The third sequence is called *salteado* (literally 'jumped'), in which the water makes a jump from the last person of sub-group A ('g') to the last person of sub-group C ('z'), so that sub-group B irrigates at night. The sequence chosen for the first turn of the year also depends on odd or even. In even years the first sequence is applied, in odd years the second.

Use of water share

From the moment the water reaches a farmer's field, his time share is counted. During the time of his share, the water user is free to use the water

Table 3: Sequences of water users within a *casal* turn

Possible sequences within the casal		04–12 h (day)*	12–20 h (day)*	20–04 h (night)*
1. Upstream–downstream	>>>	A: a–g	B: h–p	C: q–z
2. Downstream–upstream	<<<	C: z–q	B: p–h	A: g–a
3. *Salteado*	><<	A: a–g	C: z–q	B: p–h

* The time is indicated in local 'irrigation time'.

in whatever way and on whatever plot he selects. The moment that his share ends, his only obligation is to deliver the water at the point where the next user starts his turn. Because of this obligation, water belonging to the smaller shares is often applied to the plot that it is officially related to, since the time needed for the water to travel to other plots may exceed the duration of the water share. Water from larger shares may be transported to other plots which the farmer wants irrigated. In Vila Cova it is common practice to divert the water flow of larger water shares to vegetable plots for a short time, in order to shorten the irrigation intervals for these drought-sensitive crops.

Travel time of water
In Table 1 the sum of the time shares of the *casais* does not add up to 24 hours. The rest of the time is reserved for the conveyance of the water. It is composed of the time needed for the water to reach the *casal* area at the beginning of the irrigation day and the lead time between the plots within the irrigated area of a *casal*. In Vila Cova this is literally called the 'time of the irrigation canal', but will be referred to here as the travel time of water.

Vila Cova farmers have developed two rules to cope with this travel time. In some *casais* the travel time has been established as a fixed amount of time, which is not attributed to a specified water user. This amount of time (around one hour) should be enough to cover water travel time within the *casal* irrigation day. In other *casais* the travel time is proportionally deducted from the time shares of all water users. A travel time of 60 minutes over 24 hours thus leads to a reduction of 2.5 minutes per hour of water share.

For at least three reasons these rules do not resolve all issues related to the transport losses of water. First, the travel time of water is not a fixed amount of time. It varies with water flow: when the water flow decreases in the late summer period, the travel time of water increases. Second, the notion does not take into account the infiltration losses in canals and the consequent reduction of flow in more remote sections. Third, the fragmentation of time shares into portions of only a few minutes makes it difficult to implement the reduction. A faulty estimate of the real travel time, a reduction of the irrigation shares that is too limited and the illegal prolongation of someone's time share (water theft) may deprive the last water users within a *casal*'s day of their full share.

The division of the *casais* into three sub-groups mitigates the short-comings of the rules. Alternating the sequence of sub-groups means that the risk of not obtaining their full water share alternates among the users. This practice also equalizes labour input to some degree, since the first water user of a *casal* generally has a harder job in conducting the water from the point of bifurcation with the preceding *casal* than the following users.

'Half water' (Meia agua)

The summer irrigation turns last 11 days, except for the first turn, which is called 'half water' and lasts for only six days. During this turn all *casais* are entitled to only half their water share, equalling 12 hours. To create equal opportunities, each *casal* gets eight hours of water during the day and four hours at night. Only the last *casal* in the row has the full 24 hours to irrigate. Table 4 illustrates the distribution of 'half water' in 1992.

The rule on 'half water' dates from the time that demand was great for the first irrigation water directed to the *veiga*. The demand was pressing because of the rigid distinction between summer and winter irrigation. Until 24 June, all water was used on the meadows upstream of the arable land. When eventually water was directed to the arable land in the *veiga*, all water users wanted to irrigate at the same time. During the 'half water' turn, farmers irrigated the crops that were most in need of water and which would probably wilt if they were to wait for the official irrigation turn (after a maximum 11 days). Similar 'short turns' or 'transition turns' have been encountered in other systems (Hoogendam 1988).

The pressure on water immediately after 24 June has diminished since the application of water to the *veiga* area before that date has been accepted. The 'half water' is maintained, however. Including the 'half

Table 4: 'Half water' in 1992

Irrigation time	First day	Second day	Third day	Fourth day	Fifth day	Sixth day
04–12 h (8 hours)	Morgado 1	Morgado 3	Ribeira	Portêlo	Terroal	Fundo
12–00 h (12 hours)	Morgado 2	Barrias	Furado	Codessal	Talhos	da
00–04 h (4 hours)	Morgado 1	Morgado 3	Ribeira	Portêlo	Terroal	Veiga

Table 5: System operation over the whole summer period of 1992

Date	Irrigation interval	'Half water'/Full turn	Order within casal
June 24	6 days	Half water	a–z
	11 days	Full turn	z–a
	11 days	Full turn	Salteado
	11 days	Full turn	a–z
	11 days	Full turn	z–a
	11 days	Full turn	Salteado
	11 days	Full turn	a–z
	11 days	Full turn	z–a
	11 days	Full turn	Salteado
September 29			

water', three full cycles of water flow take place in every summer irrigation period (see Table 5).

The rules and practices show that transforming an allocation into distribution is a complex process. It requires detailed rules, since many factors influence the division of real irrigation time and the corresponding volume of water. Water losses in canals, travel time of water, the sequence of irrigation turns and the difference between day and night irrigation may all create inequalities between users.

The Vila Cova rules apparently prevent these inequalities among the water users despite differences in their total water rights. These rules are both inventive and simple; they create a continuously alternating pattern of water flows that at first glance seems chaotic but upon closer inspection is neatly ordered.

We assume that these rules are the outcome of historical conflicts over water distribution that threatened the continuity of the irrigation system. The rules have been defined to create a long-term solution for the conflicts. Over time, the solutions have become an integral part of every year's practice, creating a system of water distribution that avoids conflict even though water is scarce.[5]

Water distribution and the individual

From the perspective of the individual water user, some comments can be made regarding the suitability of the rules in relation to farming practices.

---

[5] Rules do not necessarily determine an actor's activities. They may be violated and need not be adhered to strictly. In Vila Cova, however, the irrigation practices follow the established rules closely.

First, several water users found the actual water distribution complicated. Younger water users were not well aware of their turns, at least at the start of the summer period. They had to consult elderly farmers about the periods that they had access to water and they complained about the fragmentation and disorder of their shares.

Second, the water distribution practices require high labour inputs from the water users. Several factors coincide. Most farmers have time shares within different *casais* and need to show up on various occasions to irrigate their plots. Also, obtaining a water share always takes more time than the time of the share, since water users need to control their predecessors in the *casal* sequence. Generally, three water users are in the field at the same moment: one who is finalizing a turn, another who is starting to irrigate and a third who is next in the sequence and verifies the time taken by his predecessor. Lastly, since night irrigation is part of the irrigation practice, every third irrigation turn includes hardship and drudgery. Using surface irrigation methods, it is especially difficult to irrigate food crops at night. Therefore water users try to swap these night irrigation turns with others who would have used their day turn to irrigate meadows.[6]

The third comment concerns the rigidity of water delivery and water use. Although water users are free in principle to use the water wherever they want, because water is allocated to a person and not to a plot, it is troublesome and in many cases not worthwhile to transport the water from one location to another distant one. This reduces a farmer's opportunities to accumulate his water shares for plots he prefers, and makes it harder to apply water at frequencies other than the system interval of 11 days. Only farmers with large time shares (around ten hours) have enough flexibility to manipulate their shares.

Two factors have increased the flexibility in water use for a number of farmers. First, a number of water-right holders no longer use their share. As a result, there is more water available for the remaining users. At present, only 56 of the 82 registered water-right holders actually irrigate crops. The water shares of the absentees are used by relatives, friends or neighbours to increase their irrigation time and to use the water more flexibly.

Second, investments in other water sources have also increased flexibility. Some larger farmers, who cultivate much land in the tail end of the *veiga* and receive little system water because of channel losses, have invested in shallow wells. These make them less dependent on the system. Two farmers have also invested in storage tanks on their plots, so they

---

[6] Some water users suggest that a night reservoir near the intake would be a meaningful improvement. This would imply changes in the physical infrastructure (e.g. enlarged canal capacities), in water distribution practices and rules (e.g. adapted to variable flow rates) and in water application methods (using bigger flow rates) and/or additional storage facilities at plot level.

themselves can decide when and how to irrigate (for instance, avoiding irrigation at night). Four farmers have recently introduced sprinkler irrigation as an alternative to the more laborious and time-consuming surface irrigation.

Conclusions

The allocation of the communal irrigation system in Vila Cova in Northern Portugal forms the basis for its water distribution system but requires operational rules that address practical issues. In Vila Cova, rules have been identified which relate to the start of the summer irrigation season, the sequences among and within the irrigation groups, the distribution of night irrigation and the water losses that occur during the travel time of water from plot to plot. The rules result in a water distribution that is clear and avoids conflict. They tend to create equal conditions for all users to obtain the water to which they are entitled.

The detail and variety of rules, which convert the allocation into distribution, point to the complexity of this conversion. This complexity is primarily due to the fact that the availability and manageability of water depend on time and space; flows vary over the year and physical conditions may favour or hinder water distribution. Second, villagers involved in non-irrigation conflicts may obstruct their opponents' exercising of water rights, since water is an important means of production. Clear operational rules and regulations may constrain such tactics. The importance of distribution rules makes it all the more remarkable that there seems to be little written information on such operational rules. The diffusion of such information may offer new options for operational changes that help distribute the benefits from improvements equitably among the irrigators.

8. Effects of a technical intervention programme on water distribution and water use

ADRI VAN DEN DRIES, PAUL HOOGENDAM
and JOSÉ PORTELA[1]

In the Northern Portuguese region of Trás-os-Montes, irrigation facilities and irrigation systems abound. In every village a variety of water sources and irrigation systems is exploited. They are owned and operated by individuals, groups or the whole community. In most villages, one system is referred to as the communal irrigation system. Such a system generally has a long history, has the greatest number of rightholders, irrigates the largest area – summer irrigation is taken as the reference – and uses the principal water source(s) of the village. These are the systems on which this chapter focuses.

The communal irrigation systems have become the object of intervention by the Programme for the Improvement of Traditional Irrigation Systems (MRT programme).[2] The programme was launched by the Portuguese Government under the umbrella of a broader programme for rural development in the region. The improvement of the irrigation systems was meant to support productive changes and increase regional agricultural output. The focus was mainly on fodder to increase meat and milk production. By July 1992 about 150 systems had been improved; up to 1996, another 100 systems are scheduled (Portela and Baptista 1985, Portelo et al. 1987, Portela 1990).

The MRT programme aims to improve infrastructure only, and has purposely excluded issues of water management from its activities. It was realized that water allocation and water distribution are locally defined and constitute complex and sensitive issues. The emphasis on physical infrastructure gave the activities of the MRT programme a rather homogeneous character; building intakes, building and lining reservoirs and lining canal sections. The assumption was that these interventions would automatically reinforce the potential for the desired agrarian development.

Recent studies have shown, however, that the effects of the intervention

---

[1] Adri van den Dries is researcher on endogenous irrigation development at the University of Trás-os-Montes and Alto Douro (UTAD), in the Department of Economics and Sociology (DES), Avenida Almeida Lucena 1, 5000 Vila Real, Portugal; Paul Hoogendam is lecturer at Wageningen Agricultural University (WAU), Department of Irrigation and Soil and Water Conservation, Nieuwe Kanaal II. 6709 PA, Wageningen, The Netherlands; José Portela is Professor of Rural Sociology at UTAD.
[2] MRT = *Melhoramento de Regadio Tradicional*.

are not homogeneous.[3] The differences in outcomes are the topic of this article. They are discussed at two levels. First, at the level of water allocation. The question is raised of how the extra (new) water is assigned in systems with different allocation principles. Second, at the level of productive changes. We will analyse what productive changes may come forward from the changes realized in water availability. It will be shown that these productive changes are partly linked to the allocation principles and their restrictions on the development of specific agricultural production patterns.

To start, we describe some general features of irrigation and the communal systems in Trás-os-Montes. In the following section the differences in water allocation and water distribution are presented. The next section analyses the relation between allocation principles and water use at farm level. This is followed by a description of the effects of the MRT intervention on the availability and distribution of irrigation water and an analysis of the incentives and constraints the extra water provides for changes in agricultural production. The chapter ends with our conclusions and recommendations.

Agriculture and communal systems in Trás-os-Montes

Several indicators point to the importance of irrigation in Trás-os-Montes. First, recent surveys indicate that 40 000 hectares are irrigated by over 1000 irrigation systems (DGRAH 1987). Second, almost all water sources that can be used for irrigation purposes – rivers, springs and galleries – are currently exploited. Investments now aim to exploit sources that could not be reached before, for instance by installing deep tubewells. Third, irrigation water is used both in summer and winter. During the summer period, irrigation complements the water deficits of up to 200 mm/month in food crop production. In winter, irrigation water is applied to meadows to prevent freezing, induce quick regrowth in spring and control the growth of certain species.

All villages make use of several irrigation systems. The most important ones are the communal irrigation systems. They irrigate up to 80 hectares. Most infrastructure is rustic; brush or stone dams divert water into an earthen canal network. Surface irrigation methods are used to apply the water to the fields: controlled flow irrigation on sandy soils and furrow irrigation on heavier soils. These methods require considerable skill and

---

[3] These studies were undertaken within the framework of a joint research programme of the Department of Irrigation and Soil and Water Conservation (WAU) and the Department of Economics and Sociology (UTAD). References to its studies may be found at the end of the book (Bleumink and Kuik 1992, Boelee 1992, Schultink 1993, Stam 1993, Verstraate 1992).

labour since flow rates are low: 20–80 hours per hectare for one irrigation turn. Field application efficiencies are mostly near 100 per cent (Rego and Pereiro 1990). In many systems irrigation intervals last up to 30 days, which evidently is too long from an agronomic viewpoint.

Shortage of water increases strongly during the summer: flows reduce while crop water demands rise. During this period the division of water is arranged via strict agreements (for an example, see Chapter 7). The division of water is based on various principles for allocation, which define the kind of water rights that exist in the system. In Trás-os-Montes four allocation principles have been identified. They are described later in this chapter. In some systems, no official arrangements over rights have been made.

Rules have been elaborated for the practice of water distribution. These rules shape the conversion of water rights into real water flows. In Chapter 7, on Vila Cova, we have elaborated these links between allocation and distribution.

The communal irrigation systems share the following features.

- Simplicity of irrigation facilities. A typical system consists of a diversion structure at the water source(s), canal(s) and in most cases reservoir(s), which are, at best, only partially improved. Distribution structures are absent.
- Simplicity of operation. In general, flows are not divided. Within the systems a single flow distribution pattern is maintained.
- Few head–tail problems. Many farmers have plots scattered all over the irrigable area(s), which reduces tensions between zones. Besides, other water sources are used to supplement the system flow.
- Minimal resource mobilization for operation and maintenance. The operation of the system is usually very clear because of the strict definition of the allocation. Collective maintenance efforts normally take place before the summer irrigation starts and normally require only one day. At the individual level, however, much labour is needed for operation, routine maintenance and sometimes source and canal patrolling to prevent water theft.
- Absence of formal water users' organizations. Within the limits set by the operational rules of the system, the driving force of the system is the labour input of the individual water users to obtain the water to which they are entitled. Organizations and interest groups surface at strategic moments only, for instance to fix the beginning of the summer period (see Chapter 7) and to decide on the future of the system, for example, improvement of system facilities, changes in water allocation or distribution.

Water allocation

In spite of their common features, the communal irrigation systems operate in quite diverse ways. This diversity is due in part to the differences in water allocation, the assignment of rights of access to water. This assignment has two aspects – a qualitative aspect: who may and who may not use the water, and a quantitative aspect: to what amount of water is a right holder entitled.

The origin of the water rights in Trás-os-Montes is no longer vividly remembered. In most villages people responded that the irrigation system had always been there, and that water rights were traditionally defined. Not one case has been encountered where people remembered the system's origin. One may hypothesize that the rights to water were created by investment in facilitating irrigation (construction works), as has been proven in many other situations. However, evidence for this has not yet been found.

Known history shows that over time, water rights in all systems have gone through significant changes. In most villages, earlier water rights were large shares, in the hands of a limited number of families and linked, in practice but not in principle, to certain plots. These large shares fragmented into smaller portions through sale and inheritance. Later, purchases of land and/or water and combining water rights and land holdings through marriage have created a diverse pattern of allocations.

The studies of the communal irrigation systems have revealed that rights may be defined on different grounds. Shares may be expressed in time, or in surface area to be irrigated, or may not be clearly expressed at all. These bases for the definition of water rights we have called the water allocation principles. They provide grounds for the qualitative and quantitative assignment of water to right holders. The four main allocation principles in Trás-os-Montes are detailed below.

Time-based: time shares

The basis for time based allocation is a fixed irrigation interval. This interval is divided into a number of time shares. During the period of a share the water user is entitled to use the entire flow. The duration of the time shares may vary; they range from several minutes to more than half a day. The number of time shares per water user differs as well. These two differences result in major inequalities between the users' access to water.

Where time shares are applied, water is allocated to individuals. It is considered a person's private property to be used in whatever way he wishes. In most systems the implementation of the time shares is however linked to plots. At the moment the flow reaches the entrance of a plot, the period of time of that plot's share starts to count. During this period the water may be applied to this plot, and to other plots as well. The only restriction is that the flow must be passed on to the next person when the time of the share is over. Only in systems with storage facilities may a person combine his time shares to use them in one single turn.

Time-based: equal time shares

Irrigation water is not linked directly to people, but is considered a local common property. Division of the water is proportional to the number of social units; households, in most villages, that claim rights to its use. Each social unit is entitled to the entire flow for a fixed period of time, which is the same for each unit. This time share varies per year. The right to the water usually depends on residency in the village. To convert this claim into a one year's water right, an inhabitant must participate in the maintenance of the system or contribute to other common interests like road or church repair. As a consequence, people who have emigrated lose their water rights but upon their return to the village may claim water again. In some cases even landless village members are entitled to an equal share, which they may sell, or use in share cropping.

This type of allocation is equal in theory, but may be subject to abuse in practice. In some villages it became evident that households with more resources sent more than one person to the maintenance activities to obtain multiple water rights.[4]

Plot-based

The owner of a plot is entitled to use the entire system flow until the plot is irrigated sufficiently. 'Sufficiently', in these cases, is socially defined: a water user may not continue to irrigate indefinitely, arguing that the plot still needs water. Irrigation turns follow a fixed order and contiguous plots are successively irrigated.

No quantitative basis

Several communal systems do not define water right quantitatively. They have specified only who may use the water, but not how much or for how long. Under these allocation arrangements, two situations are encountered frequently:

In the first situation, there are no rules at all in relation to the division of the water. This always works to the detriment of the users downstream, who may be cut off when they try to irrigate.[5] This 'free-to-take' system is found in areas where two or more systems share a water source and in areas where users from neighbouring villages depend on the same canal. This distribution of water is an expression of a weak social organization, that may be more common to inter-village co-operation.

In the second situation, that is more frequent, there are two basic

---

[4] An old woman remarked that some people receive almost all the water because they send many hired labourers, while she herself receives little water because she can afford only one day's labour.

[5] The local expression for this 'free-to-take' style of water use is *a pilha*, which literally means plundering.

distribution rules although allocation principles are absent. The first rule is that as long as someone is irrigating, he will be respected and other water users will have to wait for their turn ('first come, first served').[6] The second rule is that the irrigation of food crops always has priority over meadow irrigation.

There is evidence that in some systems the allocation principles have changed over time. Earlier changes tended towards a more detailed definition of rights. This was due to the fragmentation of land holdings and water rights as a consequence of population growth. In various systems, simple time share allocation seems to have been replaced by multi-level allocation. The most frequent result is a two level allocation where water is allocated in time shares to groups of users, and is divided on the basis of plot size within the groups (compare the two level time-time allocation in Vila Cova).[7]

Later changes seem to have taken the opposite approach. Due to massive emigration since the late 1950s the number of water users diminished and subsequently water demand decreased. In some systems this has led to a change from situations with well-defined and determined water rights to situations in which water rights are no longer defined and shift towards a practice of 'first come, first served'.

These changes are related to summer irrigation only. In general, allocation and land irrigated varies over the year. In the winter, permanent meadows, in most systems located outside the summer area, are irrigated with water from the same water source, but by a limited number of users and without the detailed rules of summer irrigation. During the winter, water allocation in most systems becomes undefined; 'free-to-take' or/and the 'first come, first served' distribution patterns are applied. When water grows more scarce, at the start of the summer season, the water allocation principle becomes vital and alive again. Only where meadow irrigation is important – for instance, some systems in the mountains – are rights as well defined in the winter as in the summer period.

The relation between allocation principles and water use

Water allocation defines the amount of water to which every water user is entitled. As such, it arranges the division of water at the level of the group of irrigators. The outcome of the allocation of water at system level, at its turn, is an input at the level of individual farming systems. The kind of share a user is entitled to partly defines what he can do with his share. In

---

[6] The local expression is '(estar) a vez' which means 'waiting until the opportunity presents itself'.

[7] Irrigation systems with a very complex water allocation have been found. Boelee (1992) mentions a communal irrigation system where allocation is defined at as much as five levels.

other words, the allocation principle of the system limits the use of the water. This is shown in Table 1, where we have indicated a number of decisions at farm level that are affected by the kind of water shares (the allocation principles). The table shows whether the choice of irrigated crops is free, whether water shares are bound to a plot and whether this water may be exchanged. In the second part of the table we have indicated the effects that the different allocation principles have on the water application at plot level.

Under time based allocations the right holders are free to choose the plot and the crop they want to irrigate with their time shares and also to exchange their shares with others. This enables farmers to apply their water on preferential plots, preferred because of the quality of soils, distance to the house, micro-climatic conditions or other reasons. This makes it possible for them to respond flexibly to crop water requirements of specific crops; some crops can be irrigated more frequently than others. It has been found, for instance, that in time share systems farmers prefer to direct part of their other shares to a specific plot growing vegetable crops.

Under equal time shares, the use of the water on preferential plots goes without saying, since normally every user has one, relatively large, time share that has to be divided among the irrigated plots. This type of allocation has the advantage that the labour input in irrigation activities is compacted: every farmer has to irrigate only once during the system's interval. The efficiency of water use at system level may be rather low, since bringing water to several plots within one's turn requires much travel time of water and causes conveyance losses in the earthen channels.

In variable time-share systems, the freedom to apply water to preferential plots implies that (part of the) water assigned to one plot is directed to another one. This freedom is often used to apply the water to more preferred crops. However, this freedom is limited in practice, since the time shares must be passed on to the adjacent plot after the share's period, and the use of the water on other preferred plots depends on the physical possibilities of passing it on. Irrigating distant plots may be less profitable

Table 1: The relation between water allocation principles and farm water use

Water allocation principles	Water use at the farm level			Water application at the plot level		
	Plot bound	Crop choice	Exchange of water	Flow rate	Irrigation time	Length of interval
Time shares	no	free	free	variable	fixed	fixed
Equal time shares	no	free	free	variable	fixed	fixed
Plot-based	yes	restricted	restricted	variable	variable	variable
No quantitative basis	no	free	restricted	variable	variable	variable

because conveyance losses are great, and because the travel time to distant plots might even exceed the time of the share when the shares are small. Consequently some users apply most of their shares to the appointed plots and only combine shares when the plots are near. In variable time-share systems, the total irrigation time of farmers is often fragmented; at different moments during the irrigation interval they have to show up to irrigate different plots. This also fragments labour input in irrigation and affects the overall organization of farm work.[8] The overall water use efficiency within the system (as compared with fixed time systems) is higher since fewer water jumps are made.

Plot-based allocation is plot-linked by definition. The water that is assigned to a plot may not be used on other plots and may not be exchanged either. This rigidity is comprehensible because the measurement of allocation is based on the time needed to irrigate the plot. This time depends on the size of the plot, the kind of crop and the water application method. To avoid long-lasting irrigation turns in these systems, farmers are not allowed to grow crops which consume a lot of water on the irrigated plots. In practice this ban concerns meadows; the contour ditch and wild flooding methods used for meadows consume much water (and irrigation time), which is not justified at the time when water should be available for food crops.[9]

In systems without a quantitative basis for water allocation farm water use is restricted only by physical restrictions such as water availability. An exception is that also under 'first come, first serve' rules, the irrigation of meadows is prohibited in the summer, for the same reason as explained under the plot based allocation. Many systems of this type show characteristics of an on-demand system. The difference is that no central control exists, so that households with more resources than others (such as labour to wait for their turn) may mobilize more irrigation water.

The sale of water rights is allowed only under time share allocation, where exchanges of water are also possible. In equal time share systems all water rights are temporary and not an individual property. This implies that water users may sell or exchange their water within one turn, or even for

---

[8] As shown in Chapter 7, water use can be made more flexible by combining water from different sources and by using storage facilities at plot level.

[9] Production for household consumption has priority in summer irrigation. In many households all available water is used for food crops. This is so ingrained in the people's minds that it appears a social norm. Even in schemes with other allocation types it will be experienced as anti-social behaviour to irrigate meadows when in a neighbour's plot potatoes or maize are wilting. This behaviour is censured by the community. This is probably due to the fact that up to the 1950s periodic hunger and abject poverty were widespread. However, irrigation practice is changing. Food production is losing importance since households have become smaller. Irrigation of forage crops is increasing to the extent that the irrigation of meadows during the night is common already.

the whole year, but they cannot sell their right to water since this is bound to their residency.

In all systems, flow rates decrease during the summer period, but the consequences differ. Under plot-based allocation, a decrease in water flow implies that the length of the irrigation turn per plot increases and consequently the irrigation interval takes longer. Under two-level allocation, where at the first level water is assigned to a group of users on a time basis, this may imply that some water users cannot irrigate during the turn of their group. Normally, this is compensated for during the next turn. Under time-share allocation, the length of the irrigation interval is fixed. The flow rate diminishes and with it the possibility to irrigate the entire plot, which tends to lead to under-irrigation.

To summarize: the principles of water allocation and related rules for distribution determine the degree of flexibility of water use at farm and plot level. The bases for water allocation have implications for land use (crops, plots, intensity) and the allocation of labour and inputs. In the next section we will show the implications of the water allocation principles on the use of the extra water that was made available by external intervention in the systems. We will also indicate how this has influenced the realization of the production objectives of the MRT programme.

Effects of the programme

The communal irrigation systems have become the object of interventions by the MRT improvement programme. This aims to expand the availability of water in the irrigation systems, both by obtaining more water from existing or new sources and by reducing losses in canals and reservoirs. The idea behind the programme was that this extra water would increase the productivity of irrigated lands and would especially increase the fodder production from irrigated meadows.

The irrigation intervention by the MRT programme was conceptually not different from the initiatives of the farmers' communities in improving their irrigation systems. Contrary to many rehabilitation programmes in so-called developing countries, the MRT programme respected the local allocation and distribution of water. The focus of the MRT programme was on the improvement of the physical infrastructure only, which in most cases comprised lining the canals and reservoirs to reduce water losses.

The overall effect of the MRT interventions is that more water is made available in all communal irrigation systems improved so far.[10] In this section we look beyond that observation to analyse the effects in more detail. Two questions are raised. First, the level of water allocation; the

---

[10] The increase may be limited in absolute terms: in 20 per cent of the cases original water flows were less than 5 litres/second.

Table 2: Effect of intervention on farmers with large and small irrigation time allocations and large and small plots

Water allocation principle	Criterion for identifying improvement	Size of resource	Before improvement	After improvement	Gain
Variable time shares	Quantity of water supplied (Q)	Long irrigation time = 10Q	10Q	20Q	10Q
		Short irrigation time = Q	Q	2Q	Q
Equal time shares	Quantity of water supplied	Larger plot	Q	2Q	Q
		Smaller plot	Q	2Q	Q
Plot-based	Irrigated area (A)	Plot size = A	A	A	Reduced irrigation time
		Plot size = 10A	10A	10A	
No quantitative? basis		Not measured	Not measured	?	?

main question is who may use the incremental water after intervention. Second, the level of productive changes; here the most important question is whether the increase in water has induced an increase of agricultural production, and especially of irrigated fodder for milk production, as was foreseen.

From our data we conclude that on both these levels there is a strong link between the allocation principles and the effects of the MRT programme. Before entering into the details it is necessary to say that the interventions have induced hardly any changes in water allocation.[11] The prior allocation principles and distribution rules have been applied to the division and use of the extra water.

The allocation of extra water
In Table 2 the changes in access to water as effects of the intervention are summarized.

Table 2 shows that in variable time share systems the effects in the assignment of the extra water among the water users are most differentiated. In such a system, water users with large time shares gain more extra

---

[11] An exception is the case of Sesmil. There, a group of water users headed by a local leader used the improvement of the communal system to change the distribution of water rights by linking the new distribution of water rights to the labour contribution of water users in the improvement work.

water than those with smaller shares. Under equal time shares, the benefits are equal for all water users. In a system with plot-based allocation, users may irrigate the same plots, but increased water flows reduce irrigation time. In systems with no quantitative basis for allocation, it is unclear how much every water user benefits from the extra water. Households with more resources than others (for instance, those with a labour force to wait for their turn under 'first come, first served') probably profit most from the extra water.

Impact on productive changes

Another important question is the extent to which the improvements created incentives for changes in water use, especially in relation to the production objectives of the programme. The overall programme essentially aimed to increase fodder production, through an extension of the irrigated area. This objective, however, was rarely attained. Table 3 summarizes the programme's effects on water use under the different types of water allocation.

Systems under time allocation, in principle offer farmers most flexibility to use adequately the additional water. The canal lining not only reduces conveyance losses but also travel times in the canals. These effects diminish the earlier problems associated with using the water on preferential plots and crops. In these systems it may be expected that farmers use the extra water in the way most convenient to them, related to the objectives and possibilities of their whole farming system.

Under plot-based allocation, water use is conditioned by more rigid rules. There are no incentives or opportunities to increase irrigated areas and to irrigate temporary meadows. Especially in these systems, few changes in the direction of the programme's objectives have occurred. Still, irrigation of plots may be intensified (by shorter time intervals). Where no definition of the allocation exists, changes in water use are difficult to predict and largely depend on the local situation.

Table 3: Effects of intervention on water use

Water allocation principle	Effects of interventions on production		
	Increase of irrigated area	Increase of pastures	Exchange/commerce of water
Time shares	incentive	incentive	incentive
Equal time shares	incentive	incentive	incentive
Plot-based	restricted	restricted	restricted
No quantitative basis	?	?	restricted

Conclusions and recommendations

The improvements of the physical irrigation facilities are a purely technical affair in theory only. The uniform technical intervention leads to variation in the distribution of the extra water in the communal irrigation systems. We have shown how the effects depend on the basis for water allocation. Since the systems kept their allocation principles, the outcome of the intervention differed, and consequently the overall gain.

Also, dependent on the allocation principle, water users may or may not be able to use the water in line with the production objectives of the MRT programme. Principles of water allocation that restrict the irrigation of pastures in summer irrigation prevent an expansion of the temporary meadows. Only in the time-based systems, where allocation does not restrict the kind of water use, may physical improvements of the irrigation systems allow intensified cattle production for milk and meat.

To make future interventions more effective and fully realize the productive potential of the system improvements, the allocation and distribution of water must be taken into account in the selection of the systems. Moreover, the interventions should aim to offer an opportunity for groups of water users to discuss flexibility in water use and a re-assignment of water rights. If the water distribution of a system is made an explicit issue in intervention, the farmers can be better involved in the planning and implementation phases and in the management changes. These modifications of the programme are likely to result in improved and more flexible water use.

9. Designing for farmer management in the Senegal river valley

IBRAHIMA DIA, GEERT DIEMER, WIM F. VAN DRIEL
and FRANS P. HUIBERS[1]

Donor subsidies for agency-managed irrigation systems in sub-Saharan Africa have been large: construction costs of US$ 10 000 per hectare and more are not exceptional, and donor subsidies for recurrent operational expenses have also been considerable. These recurrent expenses, plus the 'discovery' of farmer-managed irrigation systems, have pushed planners in donor organizations to seek to reduce costs by giving farmers more management responsibilities.

In Senegal this objective has resulted in a new type of scheme expected to harness farmer management to achieve the national goal of self-sufficiency in rice: it is known as the *intermediate scheme* by both practitioners and researchers. The name points to two features. The first is its size: the intermediate scheme is smaller than the 1000+ ha schemes found in the delta of the Senegal river but larger than the 20 ha village schemes built in the river's middle valley. The second feature is more important and concerns its management and economics. Whereas the large schemes are both agency-managed and oriented towards the sale of surplus rice, and the small schemes are farmer-managed and oriented towards subsistence, the intermediate schemes are expected to combine farmer management with commercial production.

In this chapter we report the design process for one of the intermediate schemes the Senegalese government is seeking to implement. This design process is the outcome of action research involving SAED, WARDA, and the Department of Irrigation and Soil and Water Conservation of Wageningen Agricultural University (WAU).[2] When in 1986 Senegal requested donor funds to construct an intermediate scheme near Cascas, the donor agreed to put an irrigation engineer at SAED's disposal to study its feasibility. Certain aspects were studied in close collaboration between the WARDA project, SAED and WAU.

Before describing the typical layout and management of the village irrigation scheme, we will first present the physical and human context.

---

[1] The authors are staff members of the Department of Irrigation and Soil and Water Conservation at Wageningen Agricultural University. Diemer and Huibers were seconded to the WARDA Water Management Research Project in the Senegal river valley and Van Driel to the SAED project to study the feasibility of the intermediate scheme near Cascas.
[2] The acronym SAED stands for the agency's French name: *Société d'aménagement et d'exploitation des terres du delta et des vallées du Sénégal et du Falémé*, WARDA signifies West Africa Rice Development Association.

The Senegal river valley

The Senegal river forms the border between Mauritania and Senegal (Figure 1). The river's major tributaries rise in the Guinean climate zone. The middle reach of the river starts near where the borders of Mali, Mauritania and Senegal meet, at an elevation of no more than 25 m above sea level. Between there and the sea the river flows through a 600 km long valley whose width varies between 10 and 25 km. For two-thirds of the valley it flows north-westwards, through zones with decreasing rainfall.

At the valley's northernmost point the mean annual rainfall is less than 200 mm, compared with approximately 700 mm in the southern reaches. The rainfall in the river's vast catchment area and the narrowness of the valley create high discharge peaks. The subsequent flooding of depressions forms the basis for floodplain farming. Most of the flooded area is located in the middle valley. In the off-season, the floodplain and most of the river fall dry, leaving depressions containing standing water.

Three agricultural seasons can be defined. In the rainy season (July to October) rainfed crops are grown, especially in the wetter areas. This is also the preferred season for irrigated agriculture because of reduced water requirements, low pumping heights and less bird damage. The cold dry season follows, from November to February. This period of flood-recession farming is most important in the middle valley. During this season farmers may also opt for an additional irrigated crop, usually maize. Finally, the hot dry season (March to June) may be used for a second irrigated rice crop, although the dry desert wind poses problems, as does the higher incidence of pests and birds and the higher pumping costs. Low temperatures throughout the cold dry season, and at night during the early part of the hot dry season, are also a constraint to rice cultivation.

Since the 1930s, successive governments have been attracted by the floodplain's physical potential for irrigated rice farming, which could reduce the country's increasing dependence on imports. Irrigation techniques with various degrees of water control have been tried out, mainly in the delta. However, the construction costs per unit area have been high, and the results in terms of increases in rice production have consistently remained below expectations.

The development of irrigation in the Senegal river basin has remained a major goal of national governments and has been supported by donor agencies. Over the past decade, tens of millions of dollars have been invested in two dams: one near the delta to stop salt intrusion and one on the Bafing tributary to act as a storage reservoir. The latter dam regulates 50 per cent of the discharge that travels through the valley. The consequent flattening of discharge peaks reduces the area under flood irrigation, especially in years of average or below-average rainfall. At the same time, the dam, which is near the village of Manantali, in Mali, guarantees a minimum discharge of 300 m^3/s to support year-round irrigation.

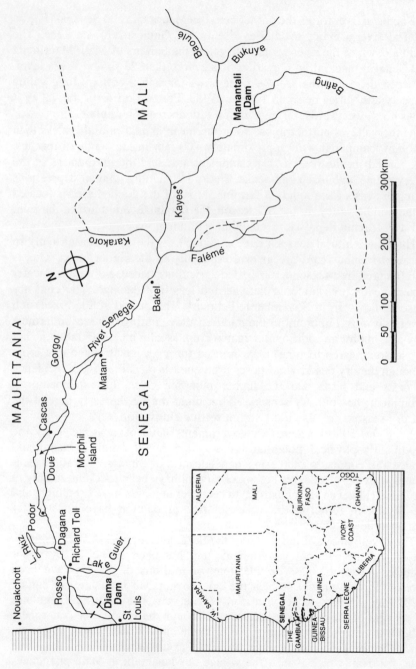

Figure 1 *The Senegal river basin*

Various groups of people live in the Senegal river valley: Arab-speaking Moors (13 per cent of the valley's population), Soninké (also 13 per cent), Haalpulaar, also known as Tokolor, (63 per cent) and Wolof (12 per cent) (Boutillier *et al.* 1962). Each group grows sorghum in the floodplain and millet on the uplands. As subsistence is impossible without access to the fields on the clayey floodplain, these fields are the object of elaborate and intricate rights that link farmers, fishermen and cattle herders (Schmitz 1986). In addition, women grow vegetables and maize on the river banks.

In contrast to the delta, where irrigation development has been difficult, slow and costly, the valley has witnessed rapid and cheap development in the form of the village schemes.

The village schemes

A typical layout of a village scheme is shown in Figure 2. A portable 20 HP engine pumps water from the river to a settling basin on the levee. From here the water travels through an adduction canal to a primary that runs parallel to the river and feeds secondaries that supply the plots. The average irrigable area of 20 ha is split into 40–80 plots of equal size. The scheme is fenced to exclude cattle.

The schemes lie on light soils that flood rarely if at all. Prior to irrigation, only the more clayey areas were farmed, and then only occasionally, for rainfed crops. The land carried bush and low trees and served as a pasture zone. Although, prior to the schemes, only small areas of this land were used for agriculture, it was subject to ownership rights. It usually belonged to one or more of the village's clans.

The schemes were in part constructed by groups of farmers who invested labour in clearing the bush and digging the canals. In most cases they lived in the same village, but some schemes have been created by associations whose members are from two or even three villages. A request for assistance from the farmers to the SAED usually resulted in the provision of a pump set, pipes, a topographical survey, a design, manned graders and bulldozers and supervision during construction. These services were provided through funds granted by donor agencies. The rare heads of clans who were unwilling to cede land were forced to comply by a law that stipulated that unused land may be claimed by people who are cultivating it or intend to cultivate it.

Farmers made these investments to solve the increasingly pressing problem of lack of land in the floodplain.[3] In the 1960s many farming

---

[3] With the start of seasonal migration in the 1930s, and of international migration of men in the 1960s, the valley's inhabitants obtained access to resources outside the valley. These migration patterns ended an historical period in which population figures remained stable through occasional massive permanent outmigrations such as Al Haj Omar's march in the 1850s to what is now Mali.

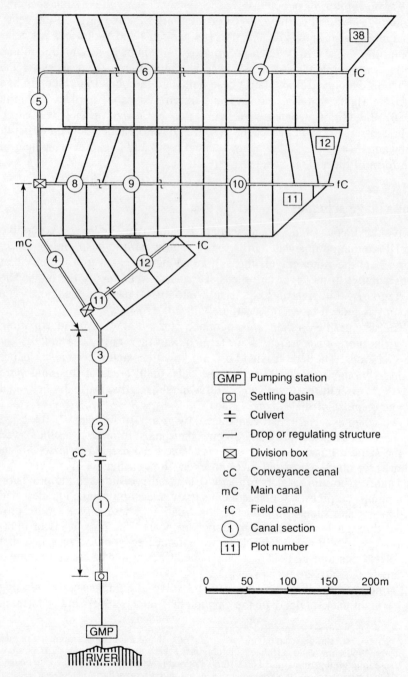

Figure 2 *A typical layout of a village scheme*

families no longer had access to the vital floodplain fields, or their fields were too small to assure their livelihood. The drought of the 1970s, when only 10 per cent of the fields flooded and only a tiny minority had a direct or indirect share in the sorghum harvest, exacerbated this trend and provided the impetus to 'do something'.

These conditions spurred some farmers to experiment with the construction of canal networks on the levees near the river. With the unofficial help of some technicians, they invented the concept of the village scheme by installing a pump and pipes to feed water from the river into the canals (OMVS 1980). Neighbouring farmers copied this idea and requested official technical assistance from their government. This help was provided with a certain reluctance, because planners had projected the construction of large irrigation schemes in the middle valley and did not wish to preclude this possibility. The President however, realizing the electoral value of technical assistance for irrigation, met the farmers' demands and in 15 years at least 700 schemes were built.

Such rapid and massive diffusion requires explanation because it is rare in the world of irrigation and, indeed, of technical assistance. It can be understood only if one takes into account several particular elements of the context. The most important ones are:

- the construction of a village scheme did not seriously damage any party, as previously the sites had rarely been used for agriculture,
- land hunger inside the villages was such that each clan head who collaborated built up prestige, whereas any unwilling head ran the risk of trouble,
- the 1960s response to population pressure – emigration to Europe – led to a steady flow of remittances that allowed farmers to pay for fuel and other pumping costs,
- the technical agencies and Senegalese and Mauritanian planners did not impose their technical and economic views very dictatorially, as they were only marginally interested in the village schemes.

The farmers invested in the schemes to reinforce a farming system that was in danger. The rice schemes were attractive because they offered the same yield stability as the flood recession fields to which many no longer had access. With the advent of the schemes, remittances previously used to buy cereals in the local shops were spent on the fuel, spare parts and other items needed to grow rice.

Production remained subsistence-oriented. This became apparent in the 1980s when the rehabilitation and extension of village schemes together with new construction resulted in a doubling of plot size. Contrary to the expectations of outsiders, farmers did not use the extended area to grow a saleable surplus. Rather, they used the new schemes to grow rice in the rainy season and the former rice schemes to grow maize (mainly for cattle feed) in the dry season.

Almost from the outset, women grew vegetables on the schemes. On the earliest schemes they sowed maize and hibiscus on the bunds. On later ones the lighter soils were divided into small plots (500 m^2) that were assigned to women. At the end of the 1980s several women's groups obtained vegetable schemes of their own, some near the river, others near the village. Here also irrigation was a response to increased water scarcity, since in many villages most women did not have access to plots on the embankment, so in the vegetable sector of the farming system, farmers 'modernized' the non-rainfed wet sector and made it more productive.

Each scheme is managed by the group that took the initiative of submitting the request to the officials and organized its members to clear the bush and dig all or parts of the canals. Once SAED, the association of future irrigators and the owners of the land had reached agreement about a site, the area to be cleared was divided into as many parts as there were members and each member was assigned a part. When the farmers had cleared the bush, and bulldozers and graders had levelled the land, the construction of the secondaries, and in the 1970s also of the primary and the adduction canal, was assigned to groups of members, as was the construction of the fence.

Members made similar contributions to the construction of the scheme. Hence they assigned each other plots of identical size and identical rights to water. The plots were assigned by lottery. (For a comparable procedure in the Himalayas see Hussein *et al.* 1989.) The rotation proposed by the SAED engineers was taken to mean that; there had to be an order in watering the plots; during his turn a member could take as much water as he desired. Repair and maintenance were organized in a manner similar to construction.

The infrastructure thus came to be co-owned by the members. As co-owners they are each obliged to do their share of the maintenance and to pay the pumping fee. Members who do not fulfil their obligations run the risk of being refused water. As the schemes pump their water straight from the river, they are independent of the performance of other hydraulic infrastructures. The scheme's performance relies on how it is managed by the board of the association. Clearly, it is vital to have a suitable infrastructure and operating environment: mechanics should be available to do repairs, there must be petrol stations nearby to supply fuel, roads must be accessible in the wet season, there must be banks to provide credit and to look after amortization funds, and stores to sell pesticides, seeds, spare parts and equipment.

The features of the village schemes that are important to this chapter can be summarized as follows:

- construction through investment of labour by farmers, albeit using donor-funded equipment,
- selection of sites that at the time of construction were rarely used for agriculture,
- pursuit of the economic objective of rehabilitating a farming system under duress,
- full autonomy for each village scheme – hydraulically, operationally and managerially.

Government policy and donor response

The expansion of the village schemes revived hopes in government circles. After several failures it again seemed possible to realize the 200 000 ha of irrigated rice that had been projected for the clayey depressions in the floodplain. The schemes were needed to feed Senegal's urban dwellers and to achieve the aim of national self-sufficiency in food. If the schemes would not be realized, the cost of constructing the two dams in the Senegal river could not be justified.

In 1981, a French engineering firm was commissioned to conduct a study aimed at developing a design concept for an irrigation scheme which, in the words of the engineer in charge, would 'associate the management capacity of the farmers, as demonstrated on the village schemes, with the economies of scale of large schemes'. The study laid the foundations for what later came to be known as the intermediate scheme or *aménagement interme-diaire*. The layout was visualized as 'grapes on a vine': a centrally-managed water source serving a main canal system from which hydraulically independent irrigation units of 50–70 ha would receive their water.

Three technical options were considered:

- constructing the main canal at sufficient height to supply water by gravity to the individual units,
- constructing the main canal at a slightly lower level, requiring a second pumping by each irrigation unit,
- using a tributary that is deepened to allow gravitational inflow from the river. In this case pumping would take place at each irrigation unit. The irrigation units would be protected against floods by a dike.

As regards the use made of the plot, it was assumed that if the government provided plots of 1 ha located on the clayey, fertile soils of the floodplain, farmers would use them to produce both subsistence food and a surplus for the market. As the Manantali dam controls only 50 per cent of the discharge that flows through the Senegal river and the clayey areas are low-lying, these plots would have to be protected against flooding by dikes. The costs of constructing these dikes are high, so their total length would have to be kept to a minimum by grouping the plots into schemes of several hundreds of hectares. This implied that farmers belonging to different villages would have plots on the same scheme.

To what extent were decisive features of the village scheme incorporated into the French engineer's concept of the intermediate scheme? Clearly, the idea of farmer management of the individual units was copied, but a comparison with some major features of the construction process of the village schemes shows certain differences.

- There was no scope for investment by farmers in the intermediate scheme, because of the impossibility of digging canals and dikes by hand in the heavy clayey soils.
- The initiative for the intermediate schemes did not come from the farmers.
- The intermediate schemes were not to be sited on locations that were rarely used for agriculture but rather on plains that still are of vital importance to numerous farmers, fishermen and cattle herders.
- The objective of enhanced agricultural production was not so much to repair a farming system under duress as to achieve national planning goals by introducing a new farming system.
- In the first two options, the irrigation units were independent from each other solely from a hydraulic point of view. They depended on each other for the operation of the central pumping station and the main canal; if a unit refused to pay its share, the availability of water in the canal would be put at risk. In this respect the intermediate schemes differed from the village schemes, which were independent from each other management-wise, because they pumped from the river.

A Senegalese request to a donor for an intermediate scheme near Cascas resulted in an agreement to implement a feasibility study for a scheme that would be farmer-managed. This study is described below.

The design process for the intermediate scheme near Cascas

A prototype design for the projected site that would resemble the schemes in the delta would consist of a centrally managed hydraulic network as presented in Figure 3.

As explained above, SAED developed the idea of the intermediate scheme as an alternative to the centrally managed large-scale schemes that had fared so poorly in the delta. It was, however, felt that the design process itself needed to be changed, to increase the likelihood that the intermediate scheme would be accepted by the farmers and would prove to be viable. Therefore, the social scientists of the WARDA research project and the SAED engineer responsible for the feasibility study agreed to collaborate. The input of the WARDA project consisted of one sociologist for 18 months and a total of 18 months of fieldwork by Senegalese and

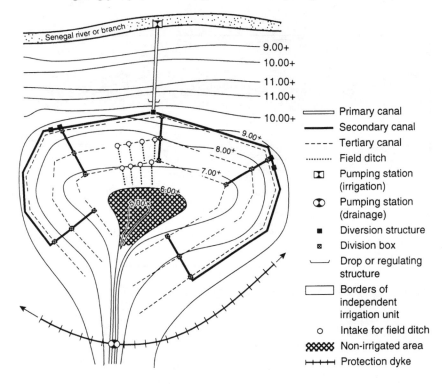

Figure 3 *Conventional design*

Dutch university students. Further input was provided by a senior sociologist and through missions by an expert from the French Organization for Technical and Scientific Development Research, ORSTOM. All researchers had locally recruited field assistants at their disposal.

The engineer required data on land tenure at the site in which SAED was interested, the size of the villages, the socio-economic, political and other links between the villages, the number of men and women interested in irrigation, the types of crops they wished to grow, and the size of the new plots.

Taking as their point of departure SAED's interest in the floodplain near Cascas, the engineer and sociologist decided that their first task was to identify the part of the floodplain physically most suitable for the scheme. The engineer was most attracted by the Mutul depression. It was decided that the sociologists would ascertain the land tenure there. To do so, one sociologist went to live in a nearby village.

Schmitz (1986) had shown that management of the floodplain was organized through *leydi*s. A *leydi* consists of clans of farmers, fishermen

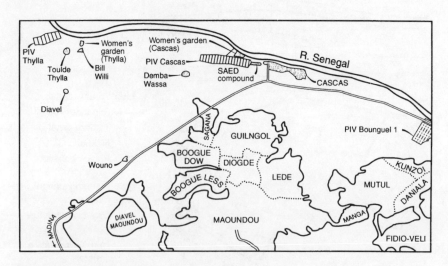

Figure 4 *Depressions in the floodplain near Cascas*

and pastoralists linked by land use rights. The farmers hold the right to cultivate after the flood waters have receded, the pastoralists the right to graze cattle on the sorghum stalks and other grasses during the hot season when the savannah is too dry, and the fishermen the right to catch fish when the plain is flooded. The Mutul site was part of a *leydi* headed by the Eliman Cambé. This person and his clan were residents of the village of Cascas. It was therefore assumed that no tenure problems would arise.

However, Schmitz's painstaking work had indicated that the depression was also *cultivated* by a group called the Sirinabé, who are transhumant Fulbe pastoralists. Most of the Sirinabé spent their time in the savannah, where they grazed their herds, visiting the floodplain only during the dry season. But a few with small herds are resident in the floodplain. These people informed their kin in the savannah who, almost overnight, sent envoys to make it clear that they did not wish a rice scheme built on the site. The cultivation of rice plots would require their year-round presence on the floodplain and would interfere with their main activity – raising livestock. The Eliman Cambé supported their position: a blood contract between himself and the Sirinabé obliged him to defend the claim of the Sirinabé against any outsiders, including the inhabitants of Cascas.

The engineer and the sociologists decided that the Mutul site should be abandoned. SAED accepted their decision, but instructed the engineer to find an alternative near Cascas and insisted that the new site also be located on soils agronomically most suited for irrigated rice.

The engineer and the junior sociologist decided to avoid the risk of further delays and setbacks by asking the inhabitants of Cascas where to lay out the scheme. After several meetings the villagers proposed a chain of five depressions nearby. These ranged from 29 ha to 175 ha in area and totalled some 452 ha. This proposal met SAED's requirements and was also acceptable to the engineer. With the assistance of a university student, the junior sociologist began to study the tenure relationships, to verify whether all relevant individuals were interested in the scheme, and how they visualized its management.

Various techniques were used. To identify basic organizational units and relationships, semi-structured group interviews were held with the members of the rural council, the village's informal leaders, the board of the defunct village scheme, the association for the improvement of the village, the association of the village's migrants, based in Dakar, and other groups. The topics covered included the villagers' view of the history of the village, the relationships between the groups inhabiting it, the relationships between the village and other villages, the rights of certain clans or individuals to floodplain land, and so on.

Unstructured interviews were held at household level. These exploratory interviews identified some questions for a questionnaire that was subsequently administered to a sample of villagers. This questionnaire investigated the importance attached by household heads to the scheme, their preferences for certain crops and their opinions regarding the criteria for access to the scheme.

The researchers learned that the village of Cascas consisted of four wards. The Guilngol ward was inhabited by two clans, the Kananbé and the Mbarnabé. Two other wards were inhabited by the Cambé and the Golerenabé clans. Due to overcrowding these four clans had spread out into a fourth ward called Tantaji, which was also inhabited by some Black Moors. The four clans each possessed their own mosques, graveyards and wells. The assumption by some SAED technicians that the wards were merely remnants of an outdated clan system was contradicted by the fact that the women had recently organized themselves according to wards to build four irrigated vegetable gardens.

The continuing political importance of the clans was further borne out by the fact that two wards were headed by dignitaries with titles. The leader of the Kananbé bore the title of 'Kamalinkou Guilngol' and the leader of the Cambé the title of 'Eliman Cambé'. These leaders stressed the different history of each clan.[4] It was found that the Kananbé, Mbarnabé and Cambé

---

[4] The forefathers of today's Golerenabé had left a village in what is today Senegal to establish themselves in a village that they called Haéré Golléré, on the Senegal river's right bank. When White Moors chased them out they settled in Cascas, only later re-establishing Haéré Golléré where they and their kin still hold land.

The Kananbé were said to be descended from animist Fulbe who had become Tooroodo, Islamic converts. Under pressure from White Moors they had left their village, called Haéré Naala, in what is today Mauritania and settled on the left bank. [Cont. over]

clans were the owners (*jom leydi*) of almost all land in the five depressions. These clans held collective (*jowré*) rights, but had allotted tracts of land to their lineages, with the latter having distributed their tracts to individual heads of households. The fourth clan, the Golerénabé, did not own land in the depression but possessed land elsewhere.

The importance of the clans came to the fore when the engineer attempted to organize meetings in the village. The clan elders refused to make individual appointments with him and insisted that if he talked with one of them, he should do so in the presence of the others. This importance was confirmed when 95 per cent of the respondents to the questionnaire expressed the opinion that not only access to land but also maintenance and management of the canals should be organized on the basis of clan membership.

Clearly, the clans would have to constitute the building blocks of the future organization and management of the new scheme. Equally clearly, the failure of an earlier village scheme had in part to be attributed to the fact that these autonomous units had had to share responsibility for the management of the central canal network.

The sociologist's findings could be summarized as follows: in spite of the administration's official view, the village of Cascas was not a single political community. It was composed of four clans that were small, more or less autonomous political communities that did not recognize any common local authority. They each owned floodplain land, but only three of them owned land on the site now under study for the intermediate irrigation scheme.

With the elders of the land-owning clans now agreeing to the scheme and in the absence of opposition from any other parties, the design process proper could begin. The designer needed to define criteria for the make-up and size of the autonomous irrigation units, the size and other characteristics of the plots, and the number, age and sex of the future plot holders. It was felt that a mix of research techniques should again be used.

First, it was necessary to decide who should have access to the scheme. The designer needed to know how many people would have a right to a plot if only the inhabitants of the village were to have access, how many land users or owners living outside the village were also to be included and to what extent this latter group were interested in participating in the scheme. Also,

---

[4] [Cont.] They were said to have arrived at the same time as the Mbarnabé. The latter had also lived in a village on the Senegal's right bank and been driven away by White Moors. The Mbarnabé, however, had succeeded in obtaining flood recession land on the left bank from the Farba Walaldé, the head of the dominating clan in the nearby village of Walaldé. The Cambé clan, which also claimed roots in present-day Mauritania, had likewise succeeded in obtaining flood recession lands from the Farba Walaldé. Some tenure claims were corroborated by the maps drawn by ORSTOM researchers.

to determine other characteristics such as the size, soil and shape of the plots, the designer needed general knowledge of the existing farming system.

If all or part of the scheme was intended for the inhabitants of the village of Cascas, their number had to be ascertained. A census that the *sous-préfecture* held in 1982 indicated 4460 inhabitants. This figure included people who lived in other villages but paid their taxes to the dignitary of one of the wards, and received food aid from him. With the help of these chiefs, the list of households in Cascas was reduced to 378 and later to 269. A sample of 67 households was drawn, representing both the distribution of the households over the wards and their distribution over the various freeborn, artisanal and slave castes. The questionnaire was used to gather information about the farming system and the contribution of the various components (rainfed millet, flood-recession sorghum and maize, livestock, migration) to subsistence and income. Information was also collected on the composition of the households (number and age of resident males and females, and of migrants), the crop(s) to be grown on the plot, the size of the plot and the degree of mechanization desired.

The farming system was investigated by one of the graduate students. He studied the physical environment (climate, soils, topography, hydrology, spontaneous vegetation), the socio-economic environment (resources, infrastructures, prices, local institutions for land management), the structure of the households (the number of 'purses', entitlements to labour and food, the role of cash), the plants cultivated and the methods of cultivation (varieties, relationships with soil characteristics, crop associations, pests and diseases, tools, use of manure, and so on).

To inform the designer as to the number of non-villagers that might claim access to the new scheme, another student made a detailed register of the rights to the land in the selected depressions. As women had begun to make increasing use of irrigation to cultivate maize and vegetables independently from men, a female fieldworker studied the role of women in horticulture and agriculture, with a view to helping the engineer incorporate the needs of these female farmers into his design. Another study focused on the organization and management of the already established Nianga, Guédé, Ndombo, Thiago and Ronkh schemes, which in various respects were comparable with the intermediate schemes as conceived by SAED.

Table 1 gives an overview of the studies conducted to determine the feasibility of an intermediate scheme at Cascas. The table makes a major distinction between the process of identification of site and users on the one hand and the design process on the other. The table also reflects the fact that a wide range of studies and techniques were used and that special attention was given to female farmers.

In his designs, the engineer incorporated almost all the socio-economic information collected and analysed by the WARDA project. He designed autonomous irrigation units in which groups of irrigators would be able to

Table 1: Sociological studies for the design of an intermediate scheme near Cascas

Stage	Type of study	Information researched	Methods
Identification of sites and users	Historical	Founding of villages, settlement of groups, acquisition of agricultural land	Interviews with heads of villages, literature search
	Identification of sites	Present uses of sites and user groups involved	Observation, and interviews
	Assessment of land rights	Availability of land suitable for an irrigation scheme according to village and groups	Interviews with heads of villages, heads of districts and heads of village assemblies
	Opinion poll	Whether groups are interested in an irrigation scheme on their lands	Meeting at village assembly level
Design	Demographic study	Making an inventory of people with rights to the site	Use of government censuses, followed by a direct survey of a sample of household heads
	Study of local political networks	Relationships between groups and villages	Interviews with informants, heads of villages, districts, lineage or production groups and local political parties
	Study of the farming system	Grain production by household; competition between irrigation and other farming activities; importance of other production goals; objectives and constraints of womens' activities	Survey of a sample of households; in-depth study of a group of female farmers; survey of a sample of female farmers
	Opinion poll	How do farmers wish to be organized? What criteria should be used to allocate plots?	Survey of household heads and female farmers

take water out of a main canal with downstream control structures without having to wait for their turn in a rotation (Figure 5). He indicated that these units should be allocated to the clans and included light soils suitable for vegetables, making them autonomous irrigation units for female farmers.

To make sure that the work of the sociologists would meet design requirements, the engineer and sociologists met frequently, both in the field and in the office. In these meetings they had to listen to each other because they were dependent on each other. The sociologists wished to demonstrate the pertinence of their training for a technical project. They were coached to listen to the engineer as if he were an informant from another culture, and look for the values and images hidden behind his words. They depended on him because he could use their sociological data only if they collected, analysed and presented them from the point of view of his profession.

The designer in his turn was dependent on the sociologists. Aware that many irrigation schemes in sub-Saharan Africa had failed, he was convinced that to arrive at a viable design, the organizational patterns of the farmers would have to be taken into account. His experience elsewhere in

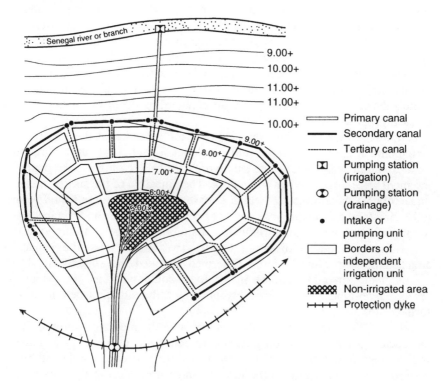

Figure 5 *Layout of an intermediate scheme.*

Africa had taught him that the relative economic autonomy of the female farmers needed to be reflected in the design. He was also aware that the layout of the canal network needed to correspond with the local political communities (wards in the case of Cascas), and that the characteristics of the plots had to be compatible with the local farming system. He realized that the study of farmer organizational patterns required sociological expertise, just as the study of the flow dynamics of the river required external hydrological expertise.

The recognition of these mutual dependencies encouraged the sociologists to discuss study topics with the designer before actually conducting the study. In this way the social scientists avoided themes that might have been interesting from a sociological point of view but which were irrelevant to the design problem. At the same time, the designer was encouraged to listen to the sociologists' suggestions for modifications to his proposals.

The simultaneous presence in the field of the sociological and physical study teams proved extremely fruitful. The presence of a hydrologist or a surveyor made it clear to the farmers that their interviews with the sociologists were linked with an intervention that could be important. The presence of a sociologist made it possible to organize meetings between farmer groups and the designer in which both parties could exchange their views. The choice of the five depressions, for instance, was arrived at after a series of meetings organized by the sociologist. During these meetings the village leaders put forward various sites as alternatives to the Mutul depression. In later meetings the designer provided information about the length of the dike that would be needed to protect the scheme, and other information regarding the physical suitability of each proposed site.

Particular care had to be exercised over the presence of the surveyors. One month after the start of the study, technicians were sent out to Mutul to do a topographical survey. The surveyors and the sociologist accompanying them were threatened with violence. The objective of the survey was to make topographical maps on which to base the design in case Mutul were to be maintained. This purpose had not been explained to the Sirinabé, nor to the fishermen with fishing rights to the site. In their view the survey was a preliminary to land confiscation. On the arrival of the team, the Sirinabé attacked the surveyors and the fishermen attacked the sociologist. The sociologist's personal standing in the local community, as the son of a respected religious leader, probably prevented the situation deteriorating further.

This incident and its aftermath, together with the meetings, showed that the sociologist acted not only as a researcher but also, being a native speaker, as a facilitator. This unexpected role needed to be strictly defined, both with regard to the farmers and with regard to the numerous other protagonists: the SAED technicians, the civil servants and the local politicians. Wishing to avoid raising expectations among the farmers, the sociologist stressed that he was not in a position to make any decisions. The objective of his studies was merely to present the farmers' points of view to the SAED engineer. The latter would be free to design as he wished. The same was made clear to the local politicians, who expressed fear that the social scientist had begun to undermine their position.

The exercise benefited from geographers and social scientists who had described the land tenure situation. The work of Léricollais (1980) and Schmitz (1986) provided two types of valuable background information – a description of access to the floodplain by different users, and of the local organizations through which the floodplain is currently managed. In addition, the two ORSTOM studies produced information about which clans held what rights to the sites under study, and about the clans with which they were associated in a *leydi*.

The design study also showed the degree of detail with which the land tenure situation should be studied. In the case of Cascas, all titles to tracts of land in the depressions were recorded by one of the university students. In the end no use was made of this inventory. Unresolved conflicts between competing claims, uncertainty about other claims, and the possibility that claims of absent lineages had been excluded made the inventory an unreliable basis for allocating plots. Instead it was decided that the autonomous irrigation units would be allocated to clans. The allocation of plots would then take place within the clans, with the provision that the plots on light soils should be allocated to female farmers.

Discussion

The design process shows that the current design method, as discussed in the introduction to this collection of case studies, is easily adapted to particular circumstances once the designer is allowed to base his work on farmers' production systems and organizational patterns. The designs also show that socio-economic data can be integrated if they are limited to the essentials and presented in ways that make them easy to translate into technical specifications.

Nevertheless, the design that emerged from the studies was considered unsustainable by both the designing engineer and the WARDA project staff, in spite of the multitude of socio-economic data that were incorporated and the numerous discussions with the future irrigators. There were two main reasons for this judgement. One concerned the expected return on investment, the other related to the management of the scheme.

It will be recalled that the dam near Manantali, in Mali, regulates only 50 per cent of the flow travelling through the middle valley. Even with the dam in full operation, the low-lying depressions in the floodplain will still be flooded regularly. Schemes built in these areas will therefore require protection. Based on a recurrence of 30 years, the dike protecting the intermediate scheme of Cascas would have to reach a height of 10.8 m above sea level. The construction costs of this dike were estimated at 536 million CFAF (US$1.98 million). This amounts to 1.4 million CFAF (US$5185) per hectare irrigated.

The construction costs of the dike were added to the conventional construction costs of the scheme, making estimated total investment costs of between 4.5 and 4.8 million CFAF (US$16 500–17 800) per hectare. Calculations based on current world market prices for rice and on the real use made of comparable schemes of one crop per year, as opposed to the projected double cultivation, indicated that these investments could not be justified.

The second argument related to the management of the scheme. Crucial elements were the dike and the pumping stations, since the irrigation units could continue to exist only if these were maintained. Maintaining the dike would have required frequent and considerable cash outlays. The costs of operating the pumping stations, one for pumping and one for drainage, would have had to be met by each irrigation unit on the basis of its water use.

This arrangement presupposed that any irrigation unit which refused to pay its share would be cut off. However, at the level of the village, there was no agency with the authority to shut off one of the units. The sociological study had shown that the village of Cascas could be characterized not as a single political community as was assumed at the start of the study, but as four such communities, and that the demise of the earlier irrigation scheme was probably partly attributable to the fact that the design of the canal network had forced the four communities to co-manage the scheme.

In retrospect, there are three main factors that help explain this outcome. All three concern the institutional context. They are the institutional background to the economic arguments, the institutional background to the farmer-management argument, and the institutional arrangement for financing investment in irrigation development.

As regards the first of these; SAED's wish to build in the depression raised building costs to US$16 500–17 800 per hectare. Such costs might have been accepted if the valley had been inhabited by a farming population which had considerable working capital, had benefited from agricultural and other training and was supported by an intricate and adequate infrastructure for both production and marketing. As it was, the valley's inhabitants were subsistence-oriented farmers. Studies on comparable schemes in the valley, where farmers had been awarded plots of about 1 ha, showed that the size of these plots did not alter the subsistence orientation of most farmers. Farmers did not exploit the technical possibility to grow two crops but continued to cultivate once a year.

The second factor is the institutional background to the farmer management argument. The demand that the scheme be managed by farmers emanated from the donor agencies, but the demand that it be located in the clayey depressions emanated from SAED as agency in charge of irrigation development. In the depression near Cascas these two demands could not be reconciled, for two reasons. First, any design for a scheme there would require technicians to operate the two pumping stations and technical personnel to manage the downstream-controlled distribution structures. Complete farmer management was therefore precluded. It was precluded for a second reason also. Some form of public coercion would have been needed to compel units to pay their dues. The units could not compel each other, as the scheme was not the outcome of a series of successive collective investments in which parties agreed to property sanctions in the case of non-compliance.

The management argument for infeasibility finds its origin in demands by SAED and the donor agency. If the location constraint were not imposed and a design further away from Cascas had been permitted, a scheme based on the concept shown in Figure 6 would be possible. Here, full account is taken of the present farming system and of the fact that Cascas consists of several political communities. As shown in Figure 6, each unit in this design has direct access to the river or to one of its channels or backwaters (*marigot*).

No unit depends on the willingness of other groups to pay its pumping dues, as each commands its own pumping station. The features of the village scheme concept that explain its rapid diffusion are taken into account:

- the units may be built with a contribution from labour investment by farmers,
- the schemes may be constructed on the initiative of farmers only,
- the sites are rarely used for agriculture,
- the schemes will allow farmers to follow their own economic evolution from substituting rice for sorghum to growing crops for sale,
- each unit will be autonomous hydraulically and in terms of management.

The scheme may therefore be expected to prove sustainable.

The third institutional factor that helps explain the outcome of the design experiment is the way in which irrigation investments are financed. Investments are financed through grants from donor agencies and through donor loans to national treasuries. Grants do not stimulate irrigation agencies to make cost-effective designs. Neither do loans, because the donor agencies make the loans available to the national treasury and not to the agency. Interest payments and debt reimbursements are the onus of the national treasury, whereas the irrigation agency is spared the costs of the loan, and even the obligation of reimbursing it. Consequently, SAED's engineers probably expected that the millions of US dollars that would go into the construction and operation of the intermediate scheme would be provided

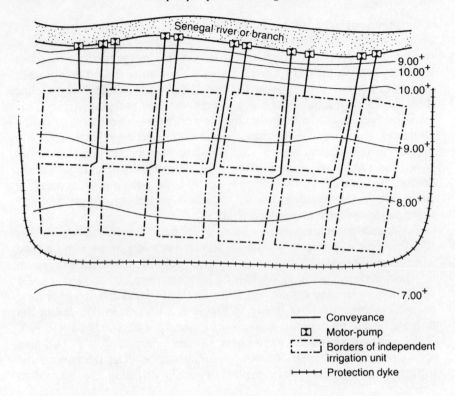

Figure 6 *Layout of an intermediate scheme located close to the river or to a* marigot

and reimbursed by Senegal's treasury. They paid little attention to the cost-effectiveness of the designs, and without any repercussions on the financial survival of their employer, they could propose designs or pose demands that would make schemes economically ineffective (compare Nijman 1993).

Conclusions and recommendations

The infeasibility of the design for the intermediate scheme near Cascas was due to a combination of demands from agencies in the public sector. The donor agency demand that the scheme be farmer-managed was incompatible with the wish of the national agency SAED that the scheme use a clayey depression. The latter preference required additional expenditure which the irrigation agency did not judge on its cost-effectiveness, probably because donor loans are normally channelled through the national treasury. Interest payment on these debts, and their reimbursement, are liabilities of the treasury, whereas the benefits of the loans are enjoyed by the national agency.

If the constraint that the scheme use a clayey depression is removed, a scheme may be designed that is possible in terms of economics and farmer management. This alternative solution shows that an agency runs the risk of neglecting opportunities for irrigation development if it views irrigation development purely as the exploitation of physical resources. It also shows that if the agency views irrigation development as the exploitation of physical potential *through local inhabitants*, it may come up with a scheme that it would otherwise not even identify.

If SAED and the donor agency could have conceptualized irrigation infrastructures as socio-technical networks, the infeasibility of the design might have been diagnosed earlier. The adoption of such a framework may be facilitated by changing the funding arrangements for irrigation development. If donor loans go to the irrigation agencies themselves, the latter will be encouraged to study the cost-effectiveness of schemes and promote technical designs that better match the evolution of local organizational patterns and farming systems.

References

Chapter 1

Adams, W.M., 1992. *Wasting the Rain: Rivers, people and planning in Africa*. Earthscan, London.

Blaikie, P. and H. Brookfield, 1987. *Land Degradation and Society*. Routledge, London.

Box, L. De la Rive, 1989. 'Knowledge, networks and cultivators: cassava in the Dominican Republic', in N. Long (ed.) *Encounters at the Interface*. Wageningen: Pudoc, Wageningse sociologische studies 27, pp. 165–83.

Coward Jr, W.E., 1986a. 'State and locality in Asian irrigation development; the property factor', in K.C. Nobe and R.K. Sampath (ed.), *Irrigation Management in Developing Countries*. Boulder and London: Westview Press, pp. 491–508.

——, 1986b. 'Direct or indirect alternatives for irrigation investment and the creation of property'. In K. William Easter (ed.) *Irrigation investment, technology, and management strategies for development*. Westview Press Studies in Water Policy and Management No. 9., pp. 225–44.

Dunham, D., 1983. 'Interpreting the politics of settlement policy: a background to the Mahaweli Development Scheme'. The Hague: Institute of Social Studies, Working Paper no. 11.

FAO, 1972. *Water use seminar*. Irrigation and Drainage Paper 13. FAO, Rome.

Jurriëns R. and K. de Jong, 1989. *Irrigation water management: a literature survey*. Working party Irrigation and Development, Department of Irrigation and Soil and Water Conservation, Wageningen Agricultural University.

Konings, P., 1986. *The state and rural class formation in Ghana: A comparative analysis*. Routledge and Kegan Paul, London.

Levine, G., 1980. 'Hardware and software: an engineering perspective on the mix for irrigation management'. *Report of a planning workshop on irrigation water management*, IRRI, Los Baños, The Philippines, pp. 5–23.

Nijman, Ch., 1993. *A management perspective on the performance of the irrigation subsector*. PhD thesis, Wageningen Agricultural University.

Olivier de Sardan, J.-P. and E. Paquot (ed.), 1989. *D'un savoir à l'autre*. GRET, Paris.

Ploeg, J.D. van der, 1989. 'Knowledge systems, metaphor and interface: the case of potatoes in the Peruvian highlands', in N. Long (ed.)

Encounters at the Interface. Wageningen: Pudoc, Wageningse sociologische studies 27, pp. 145–63.

Richards, P., 1985. *Indigenous Agricultural Revolution.* Hutchinson, London and Westview Press, Boulder.

———1986. *Coping with Hunger.* Allen and Unwin, London.

Wade, R., 1988. *Village Republics.* Cambridge University Press, Cambridge.

Chapter 2

Attwood, Donald W. 1987. 'Irrigation and imperialism: the causes and consequences of a shift from subsistence to cash cropping'. *Journal of Development Studies* Vol. 23, No. 3, pp. 341–66.

Bolding, Alex, Peter P. Mollinga and Kees van Straaten, 1995. 'Modules for modernisation: Colonial irrigation in India and the technological dimension of agrarian change'. *Journal of Development Studies* Vol. 31, No. 6, pp. 805–44.

Chambers, Robert, 1988. *Managing canal irrigation: Practical analysis from South Asia.* Oxford and IBH, New Delhi.

Ellis, W.M. 1931. *Irrigation.* College of Engineering Manual. Government Press, Madras.

Mahbub, S.I. and N.D. Gulhati, 1951. *Irrigation outlets* (revised and enlarged by N.D. Gulhati), Atma Rau & Son, Delhi.

MERS (Mysore Engineering Research Station), 1966. *Note on irrigation outlets* (unpublished).

Mollinga, Peter P. 1992. *Protective irrigation in South India: Deadlock or development?* Development Policy and Practice Research Group, Working Paper No. 24. Open University, Milton Keynes.

Nair, Kusum, 1961. *Blossoms in the Dust: The human element in Indian development.* Duckworth, London.

Wade, Robert, 1987. *Village Republics: Economic conditions for collective action in South India.* Cambridge University Press, Cambridge.

Chapter 3

ADB (Asian Development Bank), 1986. 'Project Completion Report of the Bali Irrigation Project'.

ADB (Asian Development Bank), 1988. 'Project Performance Audit Report – Bali Irrigation Project'.

Bali Irrigation Study Team, 1977. 'Bali Irrigation Study – Final Report'. December 1977

Bali Public Works Office, 1972. 'Subak System in Bali'. Denpasar, October 1972

Bellekens, Y. 1994. 'Flow Division Structures in Bali, Indonesia', in R. Yoder (ed.) 1994. *'Designing Irrigation Structures for Mountainous Environments'.* IIMI, Colombo.

ELC/ADC (Electroconsult and Agricultural Development Corporation), 1981. 'Bali Irrigation Project Feasibility Study' – Part 2, Volume 5: 35 Subak Improvement Schemes.

ELC/ADC (Electroconsult and Agricultural Development Corporation), 1984a. 'Bali Irrigation Sector Project' – Design Criteria.

ELC/ADC (Electroconsult and Agricultural Development Corporation), 1984b. 'Bali Irrigation Sector Project – Operation and Maintenance Manual'.

ELC/ADC (Electroconsult and Agricultural Development Corporation), 1985–1987. 'Bali Irrigation Sector Project' – Various Design Notes.

Geertz, C., 1967. 'Organization of the Balinese Subak', in Koentjaraningrat (ed.) *Villages in Indonesia*. Cornell University Press, Ithaca, USA.

Happé, P.L.E., 1935. 'Waterbeheer en Waterschappen'. De Ingenieur in Nederlandsch-Indië. No. 11.

Hofstede, K. and J. van Santbrink, 1979. 'Koloniaal Waterbeheer'. MSc Thesis, Wageningen Agricultural University, The Netherlands.

Horst, L., 1996. 'Irrigation Water Division Structures in Indonesia'.

Liquid Gold Paper No. 2, Wageningen Agricultural University and International Institute for Land Reclamation and Improvement, Wageningen, the Netherlands.

Lansing, J.S., 1991. *Priest and Programmers*, Princeton Univ. Press, USA.

Liefrinck, F.A., 1969. 'Rice Cultivation in Northern Bali, in J. van Baal (ed.) *Bali: Further Studies in Life, Thought and Ritual*. W. van Hoeve, The Hague, The Netherlands.

Pitana, I. Gde., 1993. 'Performance Indicators: A case of a newly developed FMIS in Bali, Indonesia', International Workshop on Performance Measurement in Farmer-Managed Irrigation Systems. IIMI, Colombo.

Staff Bali Irrigation Sector Project, 1990. 'Project Completion Report of Bali Irrigation Sector Project'.

Sushila, Jelantik, 1984. 'Development Improvement Operation and Maintenance on Subak Irrigation System in Bali'. Bali Province Public Works Office, Water Resources Division, Denpasar.

Sutawan, N., 1987. 'Farmer-managed Irrigation Systems and the Impact of Government Assistance: A note from Bali, Indonesia'. International Conference on 'Public Intervention in Farmer-managed Irrigation Systems'. IIMI, Colombo.

World Bank, 1990. 'Discussion Paper on Operational Issues at the Scheme Level'. Irrigation Sub-Sector Project Indonesia.

Chapter 4

Abeyratne, Shyamala, 1990. *Rehabilitation of Small-Scale Irrigation Systems in Sri Lanka; State Policy and Practice in Two Systems*, International Irrigation Management Institute, Colombo, Sri Lanka.

Coward, E. Walter Jr, 1986a. 'State and Locality in Asian Irrigation Development: The Property Factor', in K.C. Nobe and R.K. Sampath (ed.), *Irrigation Management in Developing Countries: Current issues and approaches*, Proceedings of an Invited Seminar Series Sponsored by the International School for Agricultural and Resource Development (ISARD), Studies in Water Policy and Management, No. 8, pp. 491–508.

————1986b. 'Direct or Indirect Alternatives for Irrigation Investment and the Creation of Property', in K.W. Easter, *Irrigation Investment, technology and management strategies for development*, Studies in Water Policy and Management, No. 9, pp. 225–44.

Diemer, Geert and Frans Huibers, 1992. *Farmer-managed Irrigation in the Senegal River Valley: Implications for the current design method*, End-of-Project report. WARDA/Wageningen Agricultural University, Water Management Project. St Louis and Wageningen.

Gandarillas, Humberto *et al.*, 1992. *Dios da el Agua, Qué hacen los Proyectos?*, Hisbol, La Paz, Bolivia.

Hecht, Robert, 1990. 'Land and water rights and the design of small scale irrigation projects: The case of Baluchistan', in *Irrigation and Drainage Systems*, 4, pp. 59–76.

Plaza, Orlando and Marbil Francke, 1985. *Formas de dominio, economia y comunidades campesinas*. DESCO, Lima.

Pradhan, Ujjwal, 1987. 'Property Perspective in the Evolution of a Hill Irrigation System: a case from Western Nepal', in *Irrigation Management in Nepal*, Research Papers for a National Seminar, 4–6 June 1987, pp. 117–28.

Quiton Daza, José, 1985. *Costumbres y Derechos de agua en un sistema de riego tradicional; Tiraque 'A' – Provincia Arani – Cochabamba – Bolivia*. Proyecto IBTA/GTZ PN 83.2073.1-01.200; Programa de Riego Altiplano Valles.

Salazar, Luis, 1992 'El Descubrimiento de la Organización Campesina a través del Riego', in Gandarillas *et al.*, *Dios da el Agua, Qué hacen los Proyectos?*, pp. 61–96.

Sherbondy, Jeanette, 1986. 'Los ceques; código de canales en el Cusco Incaico', in *Allpanchis*, No.27 Año XVIII, Cusco, Instituto de Pastoral Andino, pp. 39–74.

Chapter 5

Karremans, J.A.J. 1983. *Zon, water en vruchtbaarheid in de volkskunst van Izúcar de Matamoros; een structuralistische analyse van cultuurverandering en cultuurcontact*. Leiden, Instituut voor Culturele Antropologie, publicatie 61.

————1987. 'Irrigation and space in a Mexican community; reflections of a pre-Spanish past', in Karremans, J.A.J. and R. de Ridder (ed.), *The Leiden tradition; Essays in honour of P.E. de Josselin de Jong*. Leiden, Brill, pp. 224–35.

Ronfeldt, D. 1973. *Atencingo: the politics of agrarian struggle in a Mexican ejido*. Stanford University Press, Stanford, USA.

Chapter 7

Bleumink, H. and M. Kuik, 1992. *Aguas Mil, Towards a typology of traditional farmer managed irrigation schemes in Northeast Portugal and perspectives for their rehabilitation*, Part I & II. UTAD/DES and DISC/WAU, Vila Real.

Gonçalves, D.A., 1985. *A rega de lima no interior de Trás-os-Montes;*

alguns aspectos de sua energética, Universidade de Trás-os-Montes e Alto Douro, Vila Real.

Hoogendam, P., 1988. *El funcionamiento del sistema de riego de Illeca*, Department of Irrigation and Soil & Water Conservation, Wageningen Agricultural University, MSc thesis (in Spanish).

Stam, M., 1993. *Vila Cova, final research report*, Department of Irrigation and Soil & Water Conservation (Wageningen Agricultural University)/ Department of Economy and Sociology (Universidade de Trás-os-Montes e Alto Douro), MSc thesis, Wageningen.

Chapter 8

Bleumink, Hans and Michiel Kuik, 1992. *Aguas Mil, Towards a typology of traditional farmer managed irrigation schemes in Northeast Portugal and perspectives for their rehabilitation*, Part I & II, UTAD/DES and DISC/WAU, Vila Real.

Boelee, Eline, 1992. *Romainho*, MSc thesis, DISC/WAU, Wageningen.

Direcção-Geral dos Recursos e Aproveitamentos Hidraulicos (DGRAH), 1987. *Inventario dos Regadios Existentes no Continente*, DGRAH, Lisbon (in Portuguese).

Dries, Adri van den and Paul Hoogendam, 1993. 'Effects of intervention on water use in farmer-managed irrigation systems of North-east Portugal', in *Transactions of 15th International Congress on Irrigation and Drainage*, ICID, Vol. 1-A, The Hague, The Netherlands, pp. 181–90.

Portela, J. and Baptista, A. 1985. *PDRITM-Melhoria dos Regadios Tradicionais-Efeitos Imediatos*, UTAD/DES, Vila Real (in Portuguese).

Portela, J. Melo, A. and Baptista, A., 1987. *PDRITM-Melhoria dos Regadios Tradicionais-Efeitos Intermedios*, UTAD/DES, Vila Real (in Portuguese).

Portela, J., 1990. *Relatorio Final de Avaliação: PDRITM, Melhoria dos Regadios Tradicionais*, UTAD/DES, Vila Real (in Portuguese).

Rego, Z. de Castro and Pereiro, L. 1990. *PDRITM-Projecto de Investigação Agricola Aplicado-Metodos de Rega*, UTAD, Vila Real (in Portuguese).

Schultink, Frans, 1993. *Sesmil*, MSc thesis, DISC/WAU, Wageningen.

Stam, Moniek, 1993. *Vila Cova*, MSc thesis, DISC/WAU, Wageningen.

Verstraate, Jako, 1992. *Sezelhe, fim duma aldeia?*, MSc thesis, DISC/WAU, Wageningen (in Portuguese).

Chapter 9

Boutillier, J.-L., P. Cantrelle, J. Caussé, C. Laurent and Th. N'Doye, 1962. *La moyenne vallée du fleuve Sénégal*. Presses universitaires de France, Paris.

Hussein M.H., H.W. Khan, Z. Alam and T. Husain, 1989. 'An Evaluation of Irrigation Projects Undertaken by AKRSP in the Gilgit District of Northern Pakistan', in International Irrigation Management Institute and Water and Energy Commission Secretariat, Ministry of Water Resources, Government of Nepal: *Public Intervention in Farmer-*

Managed Irrigation Systems. Digana Village via Kandy, Sri Lanka, pp. 237–61.

Léricollais, A. 1980. *Peuplement et cultures de saison sèche dans la vallée du Sénégal.* ORSTOM, Paris.

Nijman, Ch. 1993. *A management perspective on the performance of the irrigation subsector.* PhD thesis, Wageningen Agricultural University.

OMVS 1980. *Etude socio-économique du bassin du fleuve Sénégal.* Dakar/ Saint Louis, five volumes.

Schmitz, J. 1986. *Agriculture de décrue, unités territoriales et irrigation dans la vallée du Sénégal.* CIRAD, Montpellier, pp. 545–61.